Bakelite Style

MEDIUM WAVES
200/550 METRES
LONG WAVES
900/2000 METRES

Bakelite Style

Edited by Tessa Clark

A QUINTET BOOK

Published by Chartwell Books
A Division of Book Sales, Inc.
114, Northfield Avenue
Edison, New Jersey 08837

This edition produced for sale in the U.S.A.,
its territories and dependencies only.

ISBN 0-7858-0876-0

This book was designed and produced by
Quintet Publishing Limited
6 Blundell Street
London N7 9BH

Creative Director: Richard Dewing
Art Director: Silke Braun
Designer: Michael Leaman
Project Editor: Clare Hubbard
Editor: Tessa Clark

Typeset in Great Britain by
Central Southern Typesetters, Eastbourne
Manufactured in China by Regent Publishing Services Ltd.
Printed in China by Leefung-Asco Printers Ltd.

Material in this book previously appeared in *Bakelite*, Patrick Cook and
Catherine Slessor; contributor: Gad Sassower, *Bakelite Jewelry*, Tony Grasso;
Bakelite Radios, Robert Hawes in collaboration with Gad Sassower

Contents

Introduction

In 1907, Leo Hendrik Baekeland, a Belgian chemist working in New York, invented the first entirely synthetic plastic. It was a thermosetting phenolic resin patented in 1907 under the name "Bakelite." This discovery was of profound importance and effectively gave birth to the modern plastics industry, but the popular notion that "God said, 'Let Baekeland be' and all was plastics," was not entirely accurate. We shall see that, as with all significant inventions, there was a history of essential preliminary work, carried out by others before Baekeland became interested in the subject and was able to make his unique and vital contribution.

Bakelite is a product of the twentieth century, but its origins can be traced back to the Victorian era and the development of early plastic technology. The term "plastic" comes from the Greek *plassein* meaning "to mold" and can be applied to any inherently formless material capable of being modeled or molded. In theory this covers any malleable substance such as clay, wax, and cement, but a more precise definition denotes a material which can be formed under heat and pressure.

Some plastics are derived from natural sources, some are semisynthetic, the result of chemical action on a natural substance, and some are entirely synthetic, chemically engineered from the constituents of coal or oil. All plastics, whether natural or manmade, can be classified according to their molecular structure and how they respond to high temperatures. Some are "thermoplastic" in that, like candlewax, they can be reshaped when heated up. Others are "thermosetting": like eggs, their shape is fixed forever. These plastics can be decomposed by the application of great heat, but do not return to their original viscous state. They are, in effect, set for life.

A whole host of bangles with polka-dot inserts, clear and opaque, elongated dots which have become ovals, regular shaped bangles and irregular.

Bakelite had the distinction of being the first totally synthetic thermosetting plastic.

The history of modern plastics begins with the discovery of a series of semisynthetic thermoplastic materials in the mid-nineteenth century. The impetus behind the development of these early plastics was generated by a number of factors—immense technological advances in the field of chemistry, coupled with wider cultural changes and the pragmatic need to find acceptable substitutes for dwindling supplies of "luxury" materials such as tortoiseshell, ivory, and horn. These were widely used for making a range of decorative and functional objects, including cutlery handles, jewelry, combs,

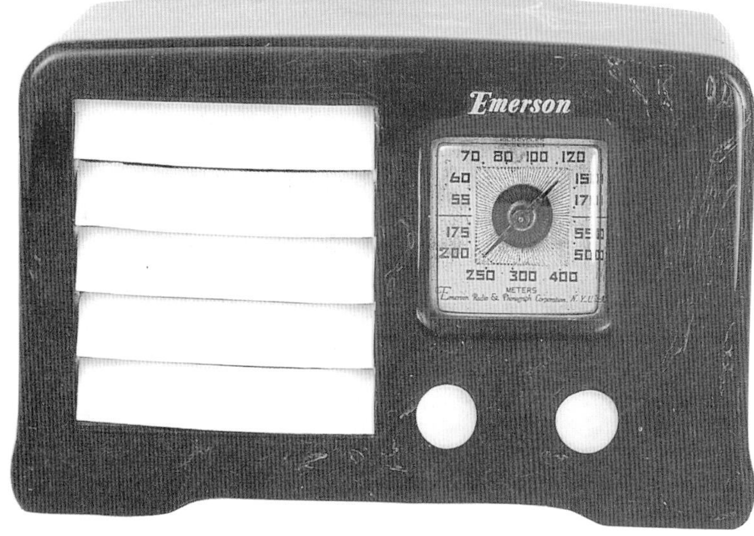

The body of the Little Miracle, manufactured by Emerson in 1938, was molded in a variety of attractive, vibrant colors, while its grille and knobs were injection molded.

This scarce and unusual radio with its three interlocking Olympic circles was manufactured by Garod in 1940.

The Wavemagnet aerial, by Capte, was mains driven valve operated and styled to look like a clock face. It has a Bakelite base with white acrylic top and dates from the early 1950s.

cigarette holders, snuffboxes, and buttons. The technique used to make objects from these natural materials, especially horn, had a strong influence on the manufacturing processes subsequently developed for "modern" plastics.

Plastics in general, and Bakelite in particular, are fascinating not only for the scientific developments that came with their discovery, but also for their (continuing) cultural impact. Bakelite, first viewed as downmarket ornamental imitation, then wonder product of a brave new world of industrial expansion—"the material of a thousand uses"—has seen this cycle of distaste and appreciation repeated. Despised and destroyed in vast quantities after World War II, Bakelite's renaissance is gaining pace, with museums, societies, and dedicated individuals collecting the material and disseminating information. We hope this book will help to foster that process.

The Baekeland Story

Leo Baekeland was born in 1863, the son of a Ghent shoemaker. After a fairly uneventful youth, he went on to study chemistry at Ghent University—a subject at which he excelled. In 1885 he turned his attention to the study of phenolics, but soon abandoned the subject

Dr Leo H. Baekeland, father of the modern plastics industry.

and turned instead to a series of experiments which explored his other interest, photography. In 1887 Baekeland patented a method of making photographic plates that could be developed under water, and established a small factory to manufacture them. Two years later, during a study trip to the United States, he accepted a post as a chemist in a photographic materials firm. After four years he embarked on a freelance career and successfully invented Velox photographic paper which could be developed in artificial light.

This discovery attracted the interest of George Eastman's Kodak Company, which bought the rights to Velox paper for a considerable sum—estimated at around three-quarters of a million dollars. Now financially secure, Baekeland installed a modest laboratory in a converted stables next to his home in Yonkers, New York, and in 1905 resumed his research into phenolic resins. While Baekeland had been busily making his fortune, some progress had been made in the phenolic field.

The years 1899 and 1900 saw the patenting of casein formaldehyde, the first semisynthetic thermosetting material that could be manufactured on a commercial basis. This new addition to the plastics family was known under a variety of names—"erenoid" in Britain, "galalith" in Germany and "kyloid," "aladdinite," or "ameroid" in the United States. In purely scientific terms,

Cast-phenolic tubes. They were probably destined to become buckles, pins, etc. after slicing and tumbling.

Baekeland's contribution to the actual discovery of the material to which he gave his name, but rather the method by which the reaction between phenol and formaldehyde could be controlled, thus making possible its preparation and manufacture on a large (that is, commercial) scale. Following a series of experiments, Baekeland came to realize that heat, pressure, and the presence of an alkaline catalyst (a substance which speeds up the reaction between two chemicals but does not join with either) were required in order for phenol and formaldehyde to combine in a thermosetting resin. Once this resin had hardened, it could not be remelted by the application of heat. It was literally "set for life." The new material was christened "Bakelite" and on 13 July 1907, Leo Baekeland took out his famous "Heat and Pressure" patent describing the method of preparation, the basic principles of which are still in use today.

In both the United States and Europe, Baekeland was obliged to take out an enormous number of patents to protect his discoveries, but although commercially motivated, he attempted to ensure cooperation, rather than conflict, with his competitors. Baekeland became something of a celebrity, appearing on the cover of *Time* magazine in 1924, listing over forty industries that could find uses for his products. In 1939, the Bakelite Corporation, as it subsequently became known, was acquired by the American chemical giant Union Carbide. Five years later, in 1944, Leo Baekeland the "Father of Plastics" died, after a long life and extraordinarily productive career.

The Domestic Market

Bakelite consumption was at its greatest in Europe and America from the mid-twenties to around 1950. In particular, the Machine Age of the twenties and thirties was also the golden age of plastics, which were widely touted by manufacturers as miracle materials that would transform the future. During this period, Bakelite was adapted for innumerable domestic purposes.

In the twenties, by experimenting with pigmentation, it had taken on a "whole new color." The Bakelite Corporation sent out an army of salespeople, armed with salesman's sample kits, containing an array of colors, swirls, and pearlescent disks. Manufacturers could now cast things in living color. Kitchens took on hues of red, green, orange, and white. Pot handles, spatulas, eggbeaters, bowls, dishes, cups, and saucers all took on the Bakelite colors.

Electronics concerns relished these new colors, because they were no longer restricted to the wood, drab browns, and blacks, to which they had become accustomed. They could now produce their wares in dazzling shades. Any family could sport a new radio in burgundy and yellow, or a new phonograph or television in shades of red and black, with amber knobs.

Picture this typical thirties routine. A couple shut off their Bakelite-clad alarm clock and turn on the Catalin radio. Then they flip the Bakelite bathroom light switch, lift the Bakelite toilet-seat cover, shower with soap retrieved from the Bakelite soap holder, give their teeth a quick brushing with their Bakelite toothbrush, lather up with a Bakelite soap brush, and shave with a Bakelite-handled shaver. Back in their bedroom to dress, they button the Bakelite buttons on their shirt, blouse, pants, or skirt. Perhaps he would insert a pair of Bakelite cuff links into his shirt cuffs, while she put on her belt with the Bakelite buckle. After blow-drying her hair with the Bakelite-cased drier, she brushes it out with the Stanley Products hairbrush. A nice finishing touch is the pretty set of red Bakelite bow barrettes.

Our phenol duo now goes to the kitchen and, as a joint venture, prepares breakfast. She whips up a few hotcakes on the griddle with the Bakelite handle. Using the Bakelite-handled spatula to flip them, she reaches for the Bakelite salt and peppers kept on the back of the stove. Her husband, having laid out the polka-dot-handled flatware, is carefully arranging napkins into several Bakelite napkin rings. They hastily toss the Bakelite dishware into the sink, the husband goes to the garage, starts the car, grabs the Bakelite steering wheel, and, with the use of the Bakelite gearshift knob, drops the car into reverse and waits for his wife.

This scenario may be exaggerated, but it does point out the role that Bakelite played in everyday life in the thirties. The cast-phenolic resin tubes, rods, and sheets by now had been processed into functional household items.

In the home

Bakelite Laminated and molding material played an important role in the packaging of various domestic products. As consumer markets expanded, rival products began to compete for attention on shelves and behind counters. Improved packaging was seen as a way to boost sales and since Bakelite could be cheaply mass-produced, it was an attractive commercial proposition for manufacturers.

Bakelite was both eye-catching and utilitarian and was quickly adapted to manufacture a myriad pots, bowls, boxes, and tubes. Widely used in the fields of medicine, cosmetics, and toiletries, Bakelite was transformed into lipstick cases, powder compacts, razor cases, and caps and closures for bottles. During the thirties Bakelite containers became familiar objects around the home. Carefully designed, often intended to take refills, Bakelite packaging enhanced products in a practical, stylish way without being associated with a particular brand name.

Table or desk lamp. A very delicate conical lamp, made of black and orange celluloid. 1920s.

Its glossy surface and wide range of colors also made it desirable for a whole variety of household items like sewing machines and needlework accessories, serving bowls, and thermos flasks.

Enormous changes in the design of kitchens had begun after the World War I, with the gradual disappearance of live-in servants and drab, utilitarian kitchens. By the twenties and thirties, they had been transformed by new, labor-saving devices, lighting, tableware, and decoration. Plastics were readily adopted to brighten and streamline utensils and appliances. Plastic kitchen goods were promoted by manufacturers for their modern appearance and hygienic properties, which were regarded as being superior to those of existing materials such as wood. Strong, self-colored plastic handles eliminated the problems of chipped paint and their heat resistance enabled entire implements to be safely boiled and sterilized if necessary. Combined with stainless steel, plastic-handled utensils could be promoted as both germ free (plastics were nonporous and therefore did not harbor bacteria) and rust proof.

In general, European manufacturers were more enthusiastic than their American counterparts in using Bakelite for objects that came into direct contact with food. In Europe during the thirties, it was common to find kitchen utensils such as coffee grinders and lemon squeezers in attractive plain and mottled Bakelite. American kitchenware firms tended to use phenolic resin more for its insulating properties, in the motor housings of electrical appliances such as irons, toasters, kettles, and food mixers. In most instances, the inner workings of the appliance would remain fundamentally unchanged, while over time new designs evolved for the casing.

Cosmetics and toiletries

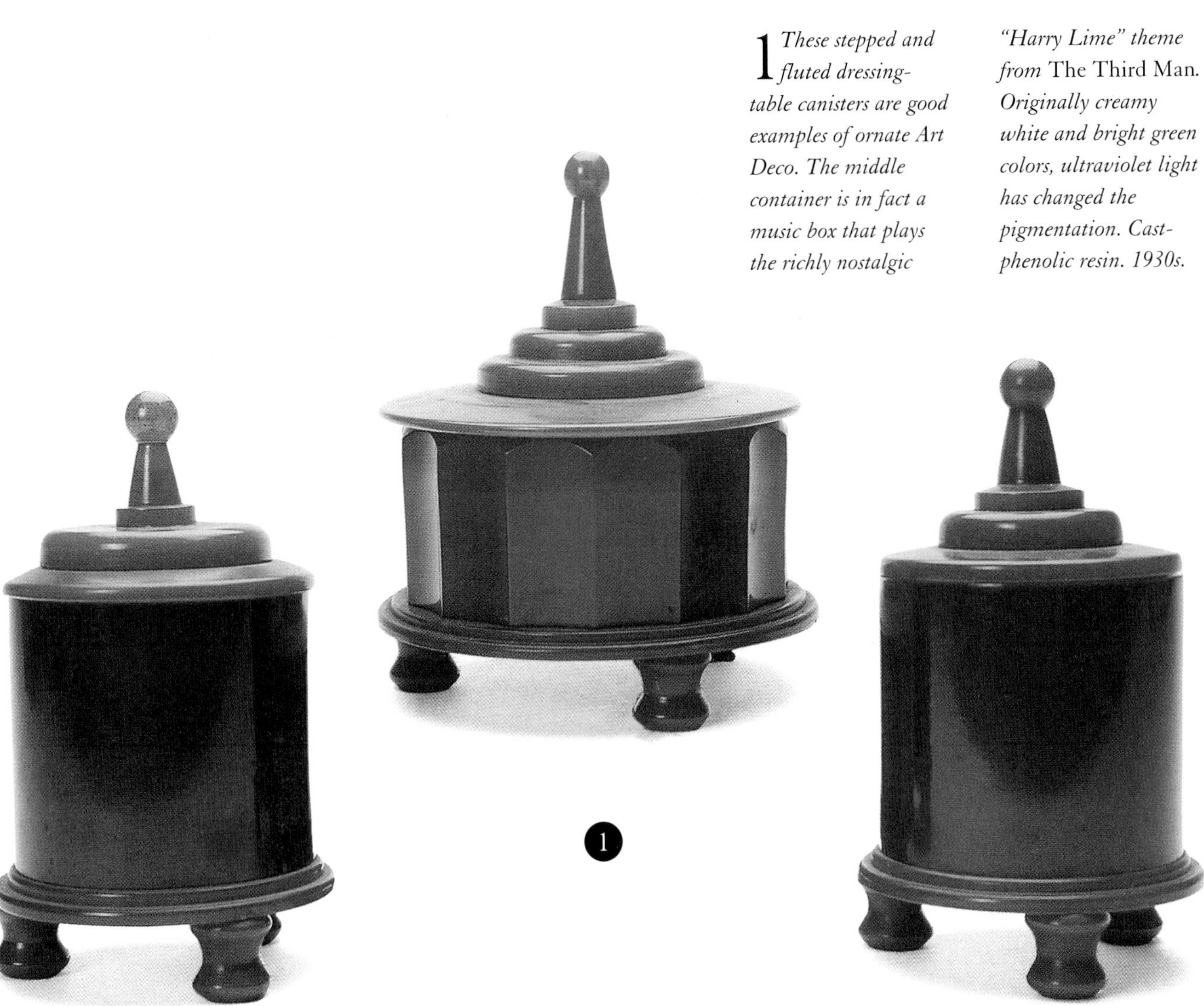

1 *These stepped and fluted dressing-table canisters are good examples of ornate Art Deco. The middle container is in fact a music box that plays the richly nostalgic "Harry Lime" theme from* The Third Man. *Originally creamy white and bright green colors, ultraviolet light has changed the pigmentation. Cast-phenolic resin. 1930s.*

2 Ebena powder box. Its unusual neoclassical shape, with stepped lid, was formed in a swirled Bakelite-type material whose bone-based recipe is now lost. The finial, however, is caesin. Late 1920s.

4 Powder box, by René Lalique. One of the most desired items on the plastic collector's shopping list, this 3-inch-square box is decorated with numerous stemmed cherries, the topmost one being signed by the maker. It may be imagination but on opening the box there seems to emanate a faint aroma of cherries. Red (also made in black) thermoformed celluloid. 1930s.

3 Rouge pots. Although it is easy to mistake the purpose of these objects, these small dice actually unscrew to reveal cylindrical containers once intended to hold rouge. Cast-phenolic resin. 1930s.

5 Powder boxes, by Ebena. These large and ostentatious powder boxes are made of a phenolic-based material over which has been applied gold leaf. Both boxes have finials, one depicting a bulldog, the other a Pierrot. The gold leaf is very delicate, and it is rare to find a box such as the blue example with its leaf intact. Late 1920s.

6 "Evening in Paris" perfume presentation boxes, molded by Prestware for Bourjois. This little collection represents some of Bourjois' inventive packaging. Each year, around Christmas, a new box design appeared in the boutiques and could be anything from a grandfather clock to a night owl. Each with their own unique bottle, they must have made charming gifts. Blue mottled Bakelite. 1930s to 1950s.

7 White's electric comb. In other words, primitive hair-curling tongs. The cast-phenolic handle was manufactured in the USA, the mechanism in England. 1930s.

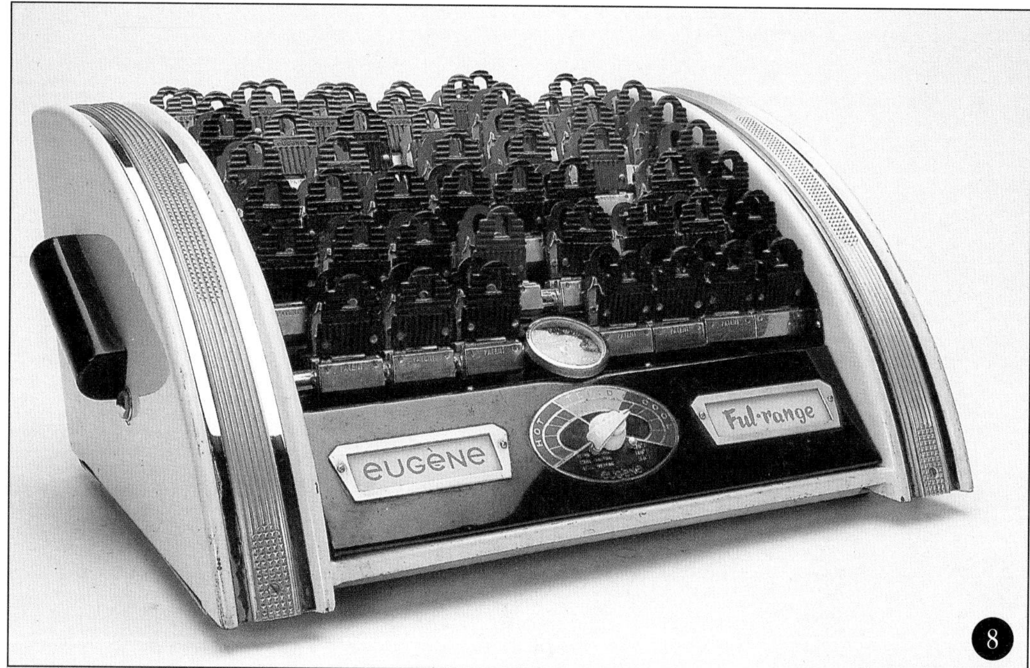

8 "The Eugene Ful Range" permanent wave machine. An ingenious machine that heated up its Bakelite-handled hair clips in order to produce those curly locks so popular in the late 1930s. This machine yet again demonstrates the robust heat-insulating properties of Bakelite. 1950s.

9 Poly double fingernail polisher and buffer. This must be one of the most obscure inventions around! Your finger-tips are placed on the bat-wing-shaped ridges located on either side of this contraption and then turned through 360 degrees by both hands. The end result is sparkling nails. Bakelite. 1930s.

Sewing

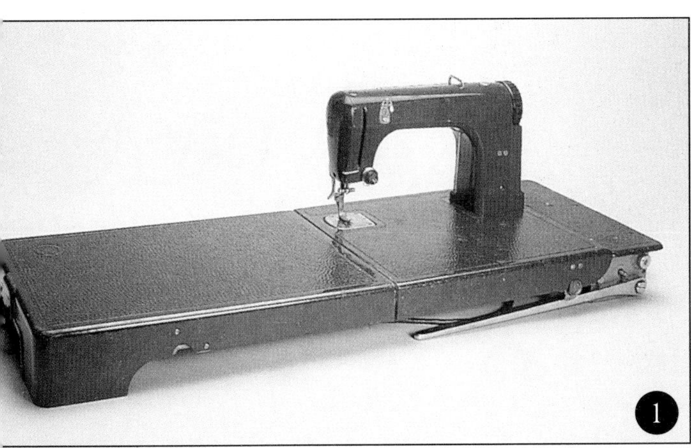

1 *Fischer News electric sewing machine. The sewing machine folds neatly into its own integral Bakelite case. 1950.*

2 *Sock darners and thimble. Some darners were operated with the aid of a 3v battery to light their tops, making the search for small holes that bit easier. Bakelite and urea-formaldehyde. 1940s.*

3 *Assorted needlework accessories. Top row from left: clear and acrylic compact sewing kit; black Bakelite needle dispenser; Miss Cutie mechanical Bakelite sock darner; and a Bakelite pin box. Bottom row: Bakelite thread-winder; cast-phenolic needle case; Bakelite thread tidy with central needle container. Mid-1930s to mid-1950s.*

4 *Tape measures. Three out of many hundreds of unusual celluloid measures produced in France and England from the 1920s until the 1940s: St Paul's Cathedral; a galleon; and—a real favorite—Sir Winston Churchill, whose tape may be extracted only by pulling on his cigar!*

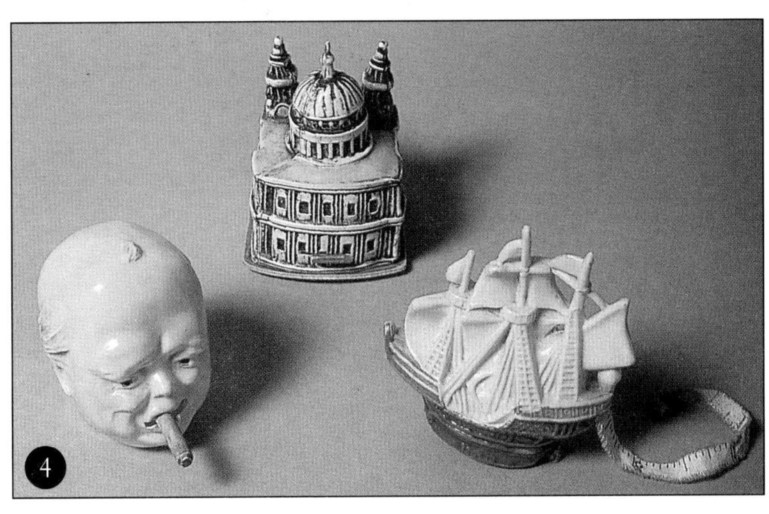

Kitchen gadgets

1 Pe De coffee grinder, by Peter Dienes. Its hinged filler cap is brown Bakelite with a black Bakelite handle. The top handle, however, is black painted wood ... Why not phenolic? 1924.

2 Bel cream maker. An age-old idea whereby milk and butter are churned by the plunger until the mixture homogenize into cream. Urea-formaldehyde, cast-aluminum, and glass. 1936.

3 Dodca lemon squeezer, Bel whisk, Hygene egg slicer, Beetleware dishes, and serving spoon. All items were manufactured in Britain out of mottled urea-formaldehyde. Mid-to late 1930s.

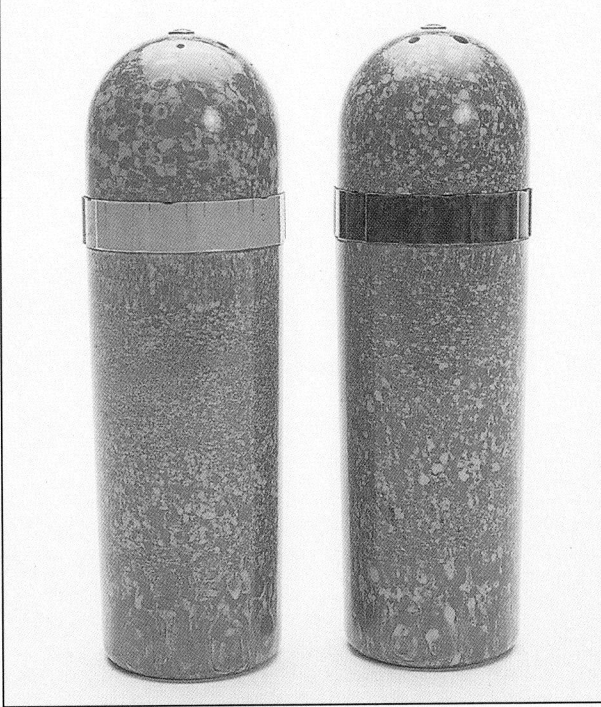

Herb or seed shaker, by BEF (its exact function is uncertain). The top of the shaker twists to select various sizes of holes. Urea-formaldehyde. 1935.

Bakelite manufacture

Baekeland's first patent of 1907 outlined a three-stage process for the manufacture of Bakelite. Initially phenol (carbolic acid) and formaldehyde (from wood or coal) were combined under vacuum inside a large egg-shaped resin kettle. The result is a brittle resin which becomes soluble and malleable when heated. ("Novalak" as this intermediate product was called by Baekeland was used as a substitute for shellac.) The phenol formaldehyde resin, pale amber in color, was allowed to cool in shallow trays until it hardened. During the second stage of the manufacturing process it was broken up and ground into powder. Other substances were then introduced: fillers (woodflour, asbestos, cotton, mica, even ground walnut shell) which increase strength and moisture resistance; pigments, catalysts, lubricants, and hexa (a compound of ammonia and formaldehyde which supplied the additional formaldehyde necessary to form a thermosetting resin). The mixture was heated to induce a further reaction between the phenol and the formaldehyde. This produced a resin which could still be melted, but only under high heat and pressure. During the final stage of the process the resin cooled, hardened, and was ground up a second time. The resulting granular powder is "raw" Bakelite, ready to be molded into manufactured objects such as radios or cameras. When the powdered Bakelite is subjected to extreme heat and pressure during the molding process, it finally becomes "set" and cannot be melted or deformed.

Electrical appliances

When Michael Faraday discovered electromagnetic induction in 1831 it was an "enlightened" moment in the history of mankind. In terms of lighting alone Faraday's discovery had a considerable influence on patterns of work and leisure, improving and extending the available hours. When the electric motor replaced steam power, the face of industry changed forever. Vested interests threatened, the gas companies quickly went on the attack. "We are quite satisfied that the electric light can never be applied indoors without the production of an offensive smell which undoubtedly causes headaches, and in its naked state it can never be used in rooms of even a large size without damage to sight." In its infancy, the supply of electricity was erratic and liable to breakdown. The first carbon filament lamps were also unreliable and had a short life. But by the end of the Victorian era technology had improved, and electricity finally won its battle with gas lighting.

In Britain the domestic supply of electricity rose sharply after the setting up of the Central Electricity Board in 1926 and by 1939 two out of three homes were customers. The rapidly growing electrical industry was the first to take an interest in the large-scale use of Bakelite, since it met the enormous demand for insulating material. In fact, Bakelite had been used primarily as an insulator in the latter years of the second decade of this century: objects such as plugs, electrical boxes, and handles for electrical units were among the first offspring of Baekeland's resin. Most of the materials used before its introduction, such as rubber, ebonite, metal, porcelain, and wood, were unsuitable or dangerous in varying degrees. Once safety standards were laid down in the twenties and thirties, the electricity industry became a vast consumer of phenolic materials for plugs, sockets, light switches, insulators, and numerous accessories. The Bakelite plug became one of the enduring, popular images of plastics; possibly due less to any aesthetic consideration than to the distinctive "fishy" smell of overheated phenolic.

Power in the home was the key to the mass development, production, and marketing of plastics-orientated electrical products. In the twenties, electricity had clear implications for the design of early consumer objects such as telephones and radios. During the thirties there was a further upsurge in the production of labor-saving electrical household appliances—vacuum cleaners, irons, cookers, food mixers, hair driers, lamps, and electric fires. In each case, "the material of a thousand uses" usually had a significant part to play.

In the kitchen

1 Bentinck kettle, by HMV. This "aero-dynamic" kettle has a cylindrical body that tapers to an electric socket (no switch mechanism). The streamlined handle is designed to protect the hand from steam. Chromium body, Bakelite handle. 1944.

2 Stella Automatic Interrupter steam maker. This mainstay of the Roman kitchen heats up milk for cappuccino, and has a cast-phenolic knob and base and chromium-plated body. Late 1940s.

3 Coffee percolator. An electric percolator of voluptuous 1940s form once again illustrates the hardiness of Bakelite when faced with tough conditions. This percolator has Bakelite handles and a chromium-plated body. Late 1940s.

4 *Burlington HMV toaster, by the Gramophone Co. Ltd. Still harking back to the Art Deco period, its design was soon to be ousted by the pop-up toaster of the 1950s. Chromium and enamel-coated metal with Bakelite handles and base. 1949.*

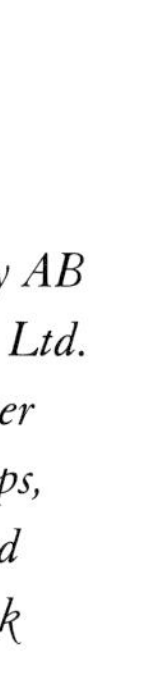

5 *Clem toaster, by AB Metal Products Ltd. A streamlined toaster with chromium flaps, whose feet, sides and handles are all black Bakelite. 1947.*

6 Maybaum toaster model 581. A toaster whose base and body are of unusually bulbous proportions. Bakelite base, handles and switch, chromium-plated body. 1952.

7 Pye toaster, by Hawkins. This interesting piece is aerodynamic in design with streamlined and faceted Bakelite handle and base, this chromium-plated toaster had a dual opening flip-over action via its single handle. Early 1950s.

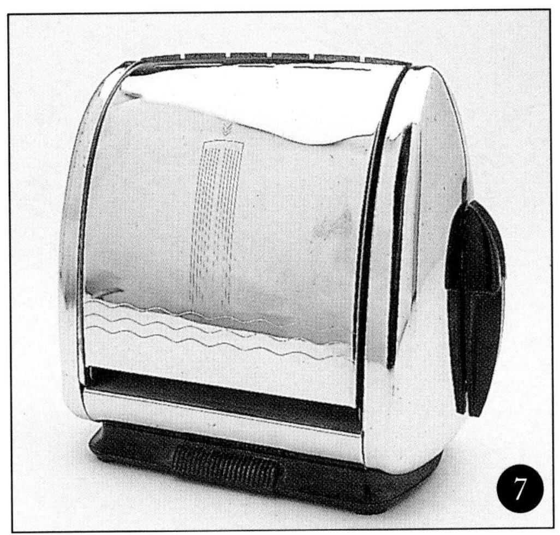

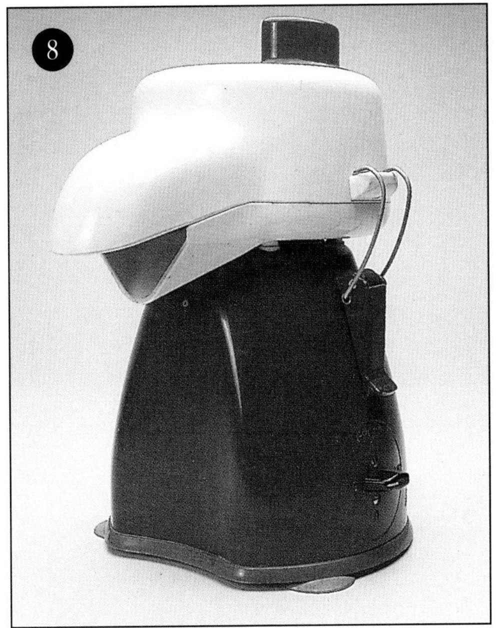

8 Electric juice press, by Riwisa. Shaped like an ugly, squawking cartoon bird. Urea-formaldehyde. 1957.

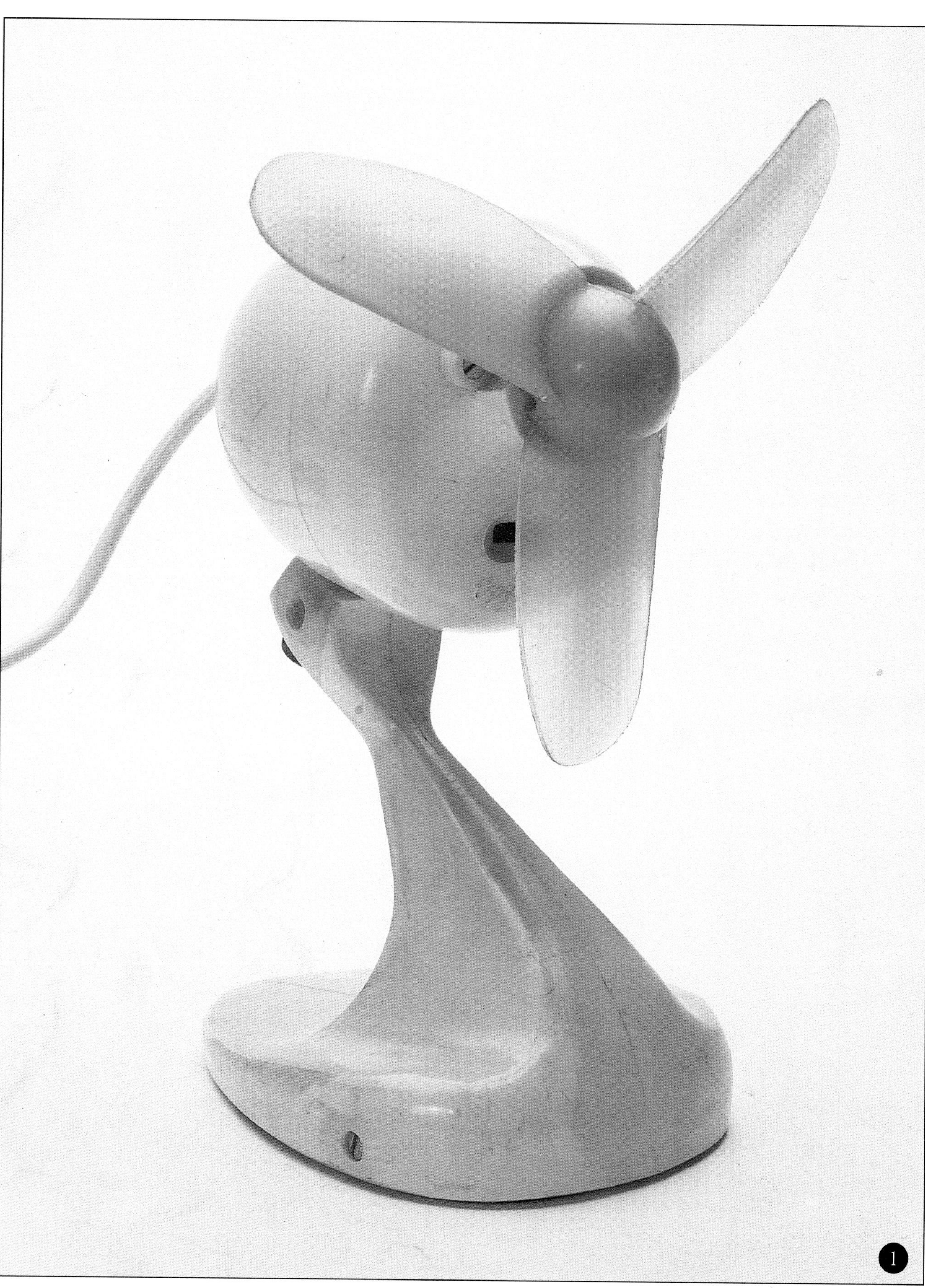

Electric fans

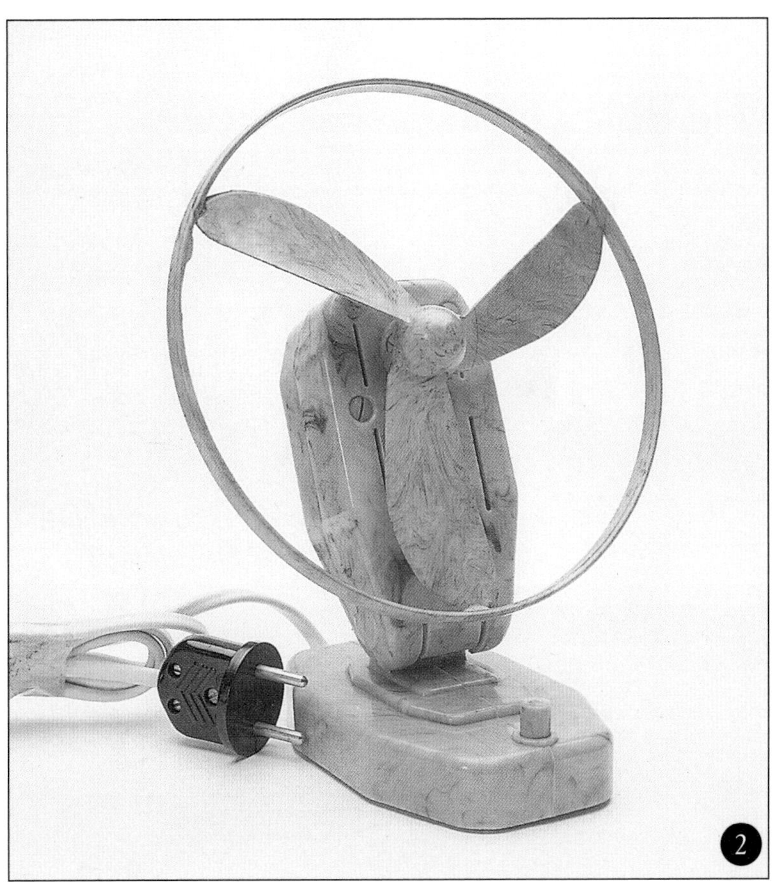

2 Microphone-style fan. The amazing idea of producing a fan in the shape of a 1930s microphone really works! Its base has molded relief instructions in four languages. Probably made of early polythene. Late 1940s.

1 The Cygnet fan, by Austin Walker Ltd. A fan with the feel of the 1950s. The body is manufactured from urea-formaldehyde and the blade blue polythene. 1950.

3 Vent-Axia Silent Six fan, designed by J. C. Akester for de la Rue. This mushroom-shaped air extractor demonstrates how function and form can harmonize within the office, factory, or home and can do so, according to the makers, "silently, economically and without draught." Bakelite with steel motor housing. 1935.

Labor-saving devices

1 Multi-press machine, by Moulinex. A really industrial Machine Age design, combining meat grinder and juicer. Polythene and urea-formaldehyde attachments with metal casing. 1950s.

2 Mixer model A200, designed by Kenneth Wood, whose company became Kenwood. This very handsome, streamlined mixer was Kenwood's first. Black Phenolic main handle and nose piece with enamelled metal case. 1948.

3 The Kenwood Chef 170, by Kenwood. "The world's most popular and most versatile kitchen machine!" It was one of the most efficient servant substitutes in the 1950s. Black Bakelite knobs and fittings. 1950.

4 Food processor, by AEG. In the shape of some enormous industrial plant. Urea-formaldehyde. 1950s.

5 Cylinder vacuum cleaners. Good example of 1930s industrial design. Though brittle, Bakelite was clearly tough enough to be employed on the household battlefront. Bakelite and metal.

6 Bustler vacuum cleaner, by Bustler Vacuums Ltd. In this early model, whose name brings the feel of cheery busyness to a mundane chore, the use of such traditional materials as wood and metal is eschewed for the sake of an all-Bakelite motor housing. 1925.

Irons

1 Early electric iron. The handle, smoothly designed for fingers and thumb, barely compensated for its considerable weight. Bakelite and chromium plate. 1940s.

2 Iron, by Prilect. A household electric iron with a lovely multifaceted, multicolored Bakelite handle and switch. 1938.

3 Smoothie, by Lucas. A travel iron of strikingly streamlined form, where the handle takes the form of fins, integrally molded with the rest of the housing. Black Bakelite and chromed steel. 1948

Shavers

1 *Travel razor, by Wilkinson. A compact and stylish razor with its own streamlined Bakelite box. Late 1940s.*

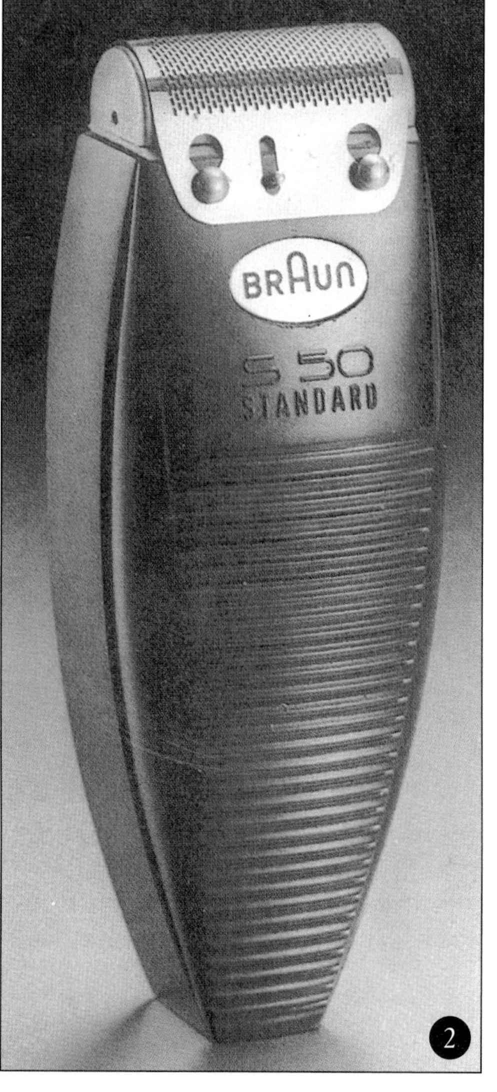

2 *Miniaturized electronic components brought major design changes to objects as diverse as televisions and razors. The bold, flowing lines of 1930s and 1940s Bakelite gave way to the leaner, more technocratic style espoused by such companies as Braun in Germany.*

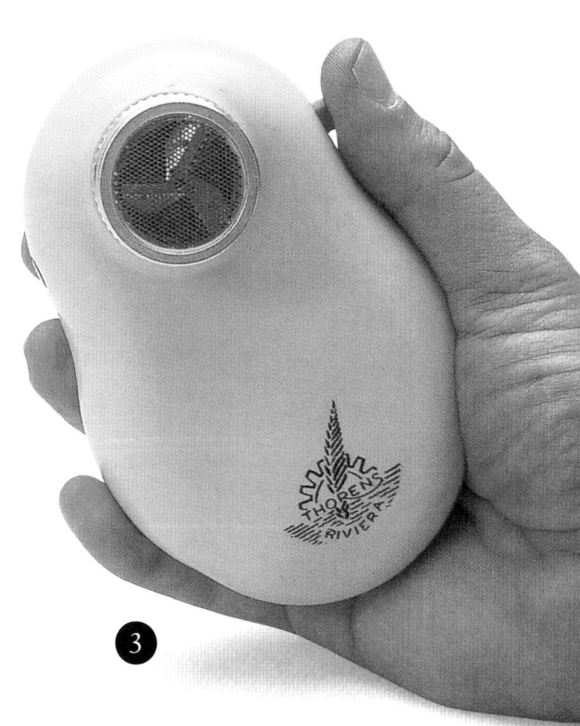

3 *Riviera Shaver, by Thorens. This mechanical hand-wound shaver is a good example of the ergonomic design of the 1950s. Polythene.*

A Machine Age material

Plastics could fully express the beauty of the new Machine Age and were the subject of many books and magazine articles celebrating plastic as a product of utopian forces. In a promotional book, *The Story of Bakelite*, published in 1924, John K. Mumford marveled over Bakelite's "Protean adaptability to many things" and the ease with which it could be molded; but found even more miraculous the chemical reaction by which it set or hardened, after which it would "continue to be Bakelite 'til kingdom come." Mumford was seduced by the idea of an indestructible material imbued with "immortality."

This view of plastics as some kind of miracle material was enthusiastically endorsed by the American *emigré* designer Paul Frankl.

In 1930 Frankl wrote, "These new materials are expressive of our own age. They speak in the vernacular of the 20th century. Theirs is the language of invention, of synthesis. Industrial chemistry today rivals alchemy. Base materials are transmuted into marvels of new beauty."

Unlike early plastics pioneers such as Parkes, Hyatt and Baekeland, who intended their discoveries to imitate more expensive natural materials, Frankl asserted "the autonomy of the media."

By the thirties it was time to recognize the revolutionary possibilities of plastics and "to create the grammar of these new materials." As a designer, Frankl was conscious that plastics were becoming more visible in design and architecture.

Two heart pins, one with Cupid's bow.

A crystal set manufactured from heat-formed imitation-tortoiseshell celluloid. Produced in 1925 by Kenmac of London, it was designed to sit on the bookshelf and needed a pair of earphones and a long outdoor aerial for optimum performance.

Telephones

It is mainly due to Bakelite that the telephone has become such a commonplace, everyday object. Before the advent of mass production, models were generally made from wood, metal (brass or steel), and hardened rubber (Vulcanite). Often decorated, early telephones were a less utilitarian and more deliberately chosen piece of furniture. Mass production brought with it the abandonment of all superfluous ornament, in the interests of saving material and simplifying the design of molds. Although telephones were first manufactured on a large scale in wood, this still proved too expensive and it was not until the introduction of synthetics, of which Bakelite was the most important, that true mass production was possible, along with a reduction of around thirty percent in manufacturing costs. Mass production was made possible by four technical developments. The combination of the receiver and mouthpiece into a single unit, the elimination of the handle, the addition of the dial, which came with the first automatic exchanges, and finally, the streamlining of the mechanism inside one casing. With cost effectiveness in mind and the demand for telephones increasing steadily, technical designers and engineers began to exploit the capabilities of thermosetting plastics.

In the early years of telecommunications the technical specifications and reliability of apparatus were of paramount importance to the telephone companies. Equipment had to be durable, robust, and require low maintenance. Inevitably the demands of mass production influenced the appearance of the telephone which became a progressive organization of components into an orderly and tactile unit. This suited the newly developed molding processes which favored simplified, more streamlined designs. Ironically, the clumsy and impractical "candlestick" or pedestal telephone, dating from 1900, was considered streamlined in its day and remained standard office equipment for around twenty-five years.

In 1927 the Bell Telephone Company, established by the inventor Alexander Graham Bell, developed a handset in black phenolic resin, but the design was bulky and uncomfortable to use. Bell sought out the American industrial designer Henry Dreyfuss and delivered his famous request to provide "a little art to wrap the telephone in." Whilst Dreyfuss redesigned the external appearance, Bell's engineers were working to modify the internal mechanism. The resulting black phenolic casing appeared in 1937. It was more compact and represented a definite technical improvement, but the receiver was still too heavy, sat uncomfortably on its cradle and the dial was difficult to keep clean. In 1950 Dreyfuss redesigned the telephone in lightweight thermoplastic. Still in common use today, this model was durable, streamlined, easy to clean, with a much improved receiver design, which meant that it was less inclined to jump off the hook.

Bakelite was first used for telephones in America and then spread to Europe. In the Netherlands, the first all-Bakelite telephone appeared in 1931, made by the Ericsson Telefoon company. The Netherlands Post Office greatly approved of Bakelite because of its durability and robustness, which obviated the need for constant replacement of parts.

1 GPO (General Post Office) 332 Series telephone. The first telephone designed in Britain with a built-in bell, it proved to be an extremely robust design and was still in use well into the 1960s. Available in black Bakelite. In the late 1940s, this telephone was also produced in ivory, green, and red acrylic. 1936.

1

2 GPO (General Post Office) 162 Series telephone. The first telephone to have the handset resting on the body of the telephone, it was known in the trade as the "hand combination set." It was also the first telephone made entirely of plastic. A mottled "walnut" prototype, now extremely rare, was superseded by versions in black Bakelite, and ivory, red, and green urea-formaldehyde—all of which are desirable today. 1929.

In the Netherlands during the thirties, there was a proliferation of different telephone designs all manufactured in black Bakelite. Parts were not generally interchangeable, which created a certain amount of confusion and waste. By the end of the forties there was a growing need for standardization and the Netherlands Post Office responded by developing the first "universal telephone" in collaboration with a single manufacturer. Some rogue models still persisted, but black remained the universal color until Ericsson Telefoon brought out a white urea model in 1954. Complete standardization was eventually achieved in 1965, with a gray model half the weight of its Bakelite predecessor.

In Britain, the GPO, following the Dutch example, began to specify the use of phenolic plastics for standard-issue black telephones. For colored telephones, acrylic plastics were chosen—red and green telephones were made of Diakon. Different materials were explored to emphasize durability and color intensity. From a collector's point of view, there is considerable variation in these colors. Cream telephones ranged in color and texture from almost white to a rich ivory. Direct sunlight affected the color of the red telephones, soon turning them a salmon pink. There were various experiments to achieve a permanent blue. Legend has it that a batch of royal blue telephones was given a trial run by the British monarchy at Buckingham Palace, but this has never been officially confirmed! Brown Bakelite telephones (Type 301) are also considered a rarity—they have a distinctive "walnut" finish which exploits the imitative character of the material.

3 *The Ericophon telephone, designed by Gosta Thomas. It remains a classic example of the freedom to explore organic forms made possible by new plastics technology. 1954.*

4 *SNCT (Société National de Communication Téléfonique) telephone. Found in numerous French homes in the 1940s. Made in either brown or black Bakelite.*

From tables to time

1 *Napkin rings in various stylized animal forms with inset semitransparent eyes. These were sold either individually or in large extruded tubes of cast-phenolic resin. The rocking horse is rare, and all are quite collectible. 1940s and 1950s.*

2 *One can only assume that these were decorative and not, as it would seem, for transporting your napkins across the table. Cast-phenolic resin with polythene wheels. Early 1950s.*

Manufacturers of the earliest plastic goods were essentially businessmen with a desire to satisfy popular taste. Their products were in no sense "designed"—rather they were imitations of the prevailing Victorian and Edwardian styles of ornament that dominated the late nineteenth and early twentieth centuries. Like any new material, Bakelite began with designs based on existing models—fruit bowls with thin sides like porcelain, or thick sides like glass; radio cabinets in imitation walnut and clock cases which reproduced existing metal or wooden examples. This imitative character is also noticeable in Bakelite objects made in the Art Deco style: motifs such as the fan, sun ray, fountain, wave, and zigzag are frequently found in early Bakelite clocks, the designs of which are based on wooden originals.

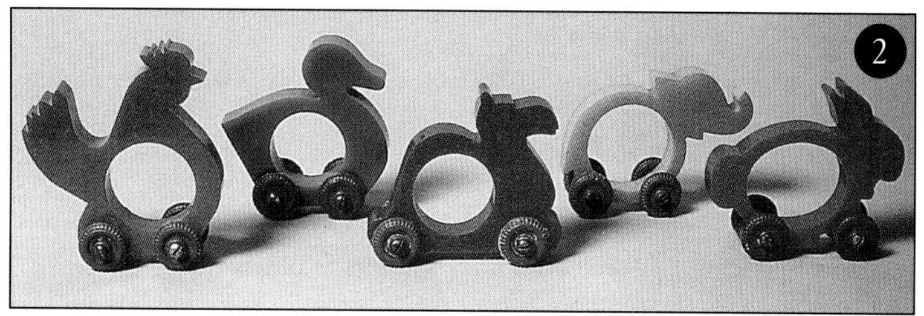

For tableware (and kitchenware), phenolic materials were gradually superseded by urea-formaldehyde resins, which appeared less heavy and somber and also had a much greater color range. Urea-formaldehyde was often known as "Beetleware" and was used extensively to produce dinner plates, bowls, and picnic sets in light and mottled colors. The latter effect was often achieved by grinding different-colored batches of material to varying degrees of fineness before mixing them in the mold, with the result that they combined imperfectly to create the marbleized finish that is characteristic of much plastic tableware. British manufacturers of Beetleware included Brookes and Adams (who made distinctive marbled "Bandalastaware") and GEC. Despite being a modern material, urea dinner and picnic sets tended to emulate the traditional designs of china tableware—the crucial difference being that the plastic was unbreakable, a point manufacturers were always keen to emphasize.

Furniture, too, was manufactured in plastic as designers responded to the potential of this new material, which was not only cost effective and pleasing aesthetically, but which allowed them to experiment with new shapes that were impossible to achieve with traditional materials like wood.

Tableware

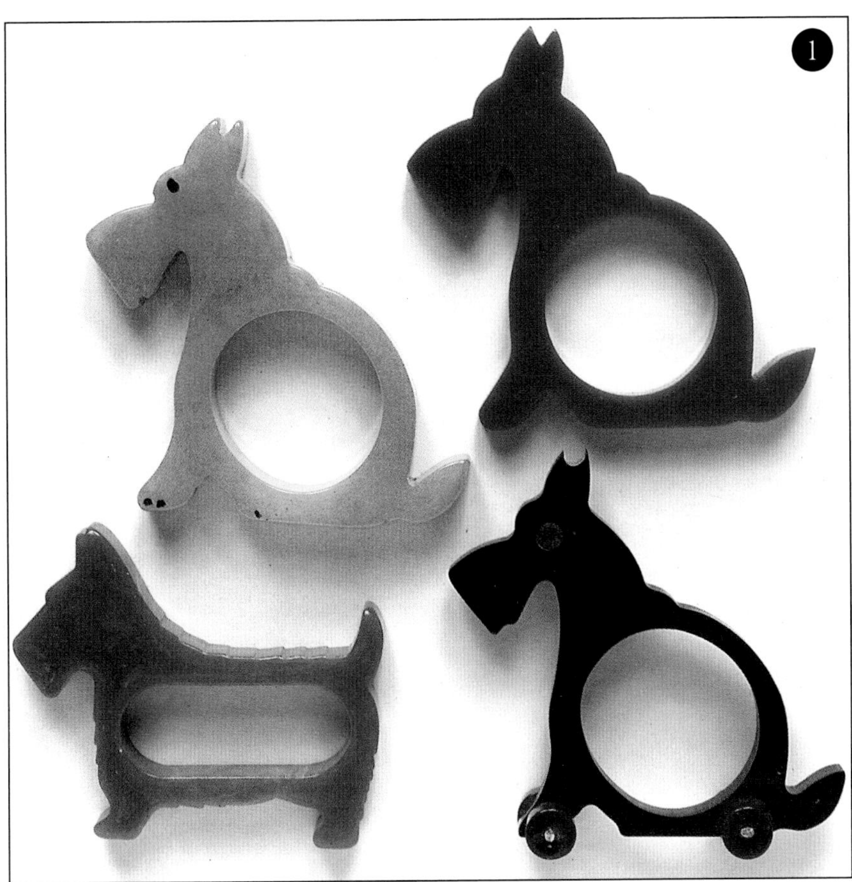

1 *Bakelite napkin rings, one with wheels. These have remained immensely popular to this day, particularly in Europe.*

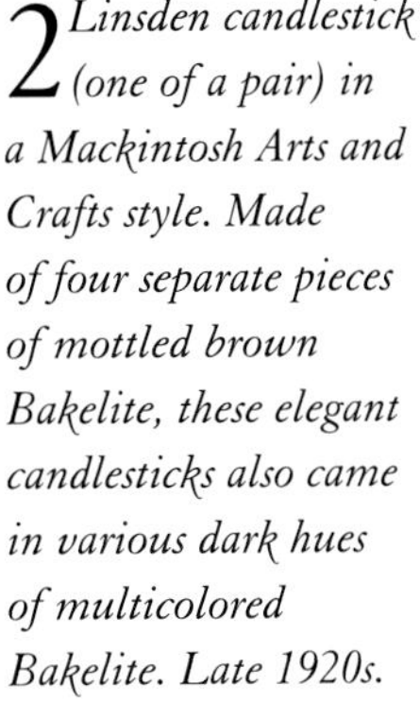

2 *Linsden candlestick (one of a pair) in a Mackintosh Arts and Crafts style. Made of four separate pieces of mottled brown Bakelite, these elegant candlesticks also came in various dark hues of multicolored Bakelite. Late 1920s.*

3 Sorbet dish, spoon, Easter-egg cases, and a sundae cup. The effect of this assortment of simple but attractive multi-colored moldings is strongly imitative of polished stone. Urea-formaldehyde. 1940s.

4 Bourn-Vita sleeping beakers, by Cadbury's. These cups are the quintessence of 1950s style. The beaker's nightcap acts as a lid to keep the hot chocolate warm. Once only available with Cadbury's coupons, these cups are becoming increasingly popular today. Urea-formaldehyde body and nightcap, cellulose acetate bobble. 1951.

Molding and casting Bakelite

Among the several molding processes employed for the manufacture of Bakelite objects, compression molding became one of the most commonly used. During compression molding raw Bakelite (in powder or pellet form) was placed inside a mold and subjected to extreme pressure at high temperature. The size of the object was generally limited by the levels of heat and pressure required, while the need to achieve an even rate of hardening also limited the thickness of the object's sides. However, one advantage of compression molding was the range of color that could be achieved. It was possible to add more color during the molding process, either to enhance or create color gradations. Being inherently dark in color, Bakelite could therefore be easily "modified" to mimic the appearance of other materials such as wood, marble, ceramics, horn, or amber.

Two other manufacturing methods were transfer molding and injection molding, which are essentially quite similar, in that molten Bakelite is squeezed through a narrow duct into a closed mold. These methods generally resulted in fewer "flash" lines, that is, lines of excess material along joins in the mold which must eventually be filed away. Although faster than compression molding, neither method allowed the combination of colors on the surface of a single object.

In some cases, objects were cast instead of molded. During the casting process, the viscous phenolic material was simply poured into a lead mold and allowed to harden slowly. Cast-phenolic resin (now rarely produced) had more or less the same ingredients as molding resin, but by subtly varying the base mixture and adding coloring agents, it could be produced in a much greater range of colors. These included white, pastels, and vivid "jewel-like" hues. If filling agents were omitted, the cast resin could be transparent or translucent. Other effects, such as mottling, could be created by stirring a special substance into the resin before it was poured into the lead molds. Finished castings often took the form of rods, cylinders, and letters of the alphabet, from which lettering for signs was made. Cast Bakelite was also used extensively to make buttons and costume jewelry. Other methods used for processing Bakelite included extrusion, to produce rods and bars of unlimited length, and lamination, whereby sheets of fabric or paper were coated with resin and then bonded together under heat and pressure. Bakelite could also be molded without high pressure—in this case extra gas was added to make the material foam and the result is a cellular, fire-resistant material, ideal for insulation.

Toast rack. Made of thick thiourea-formaldehyde, unmarked. 1930s.

Furniture

1 Paul T. Frankl's red lacquered puzzle desk, which looks back to Oriental forms. The designer went on to become an enthusiastic disciple of the miracle substance: plastics. "These new materials are expressive of our own age. They speak in the vernacular of the twentieth century."

3 Electric fireplace. This fireplace shows a startling clash between modern and traditional inspirations. The imitation-tile effect and attempt to evoke stone or marble shapes in the lower section, as well as the combination of electric barheaters and fake grate, underline the uncertainty of this design. Bakelite. 1930s.

2 Cabriolet-legged Bakelite sidetable with an assortment of boxes. It is hard to imagine a greater contrast between the kitsch exuberance we tend to associate with early plastics, as seen in these four boxes, and the po-faced absurdity of the postware "plastic Chippendale" they sit on.

Clocks and watches

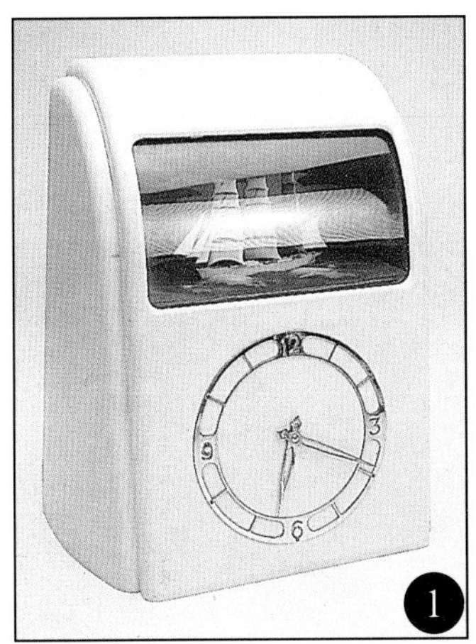

1 *This curious-looking object, known as a "vitascope," is an electric clock incorporating a galleon that bobs up and down in front of a rising and setting sun. The effect is mildly soporific and fulfils its intended function as a night light. Made in the Isle of Man in the late 1940s and early 1950s, the housing is available in either Bakelite or Perspex.*

2 *JAZ alarm clock. The French company JAZ made many Bakelite clocks during the 1930s and 1940s, all of which should be on the collector's want list. This example is inset with frosted-glass panels showing ladies in Lalique-style costume.*

3 *"Electric" alarm clock, in an unusual Gothic style. Made of textured Bakelite. 1940s.*

4 *A clock shaped like the car headlamp to be found on an Austin car of the 1930s. Bakelite and brass. 1930s.*

5 Smith's Sectric. An electric alarm clock produced in vast quantities in Britain during the early 1950s. Made in various pastel shades of urea-formaldehyde.

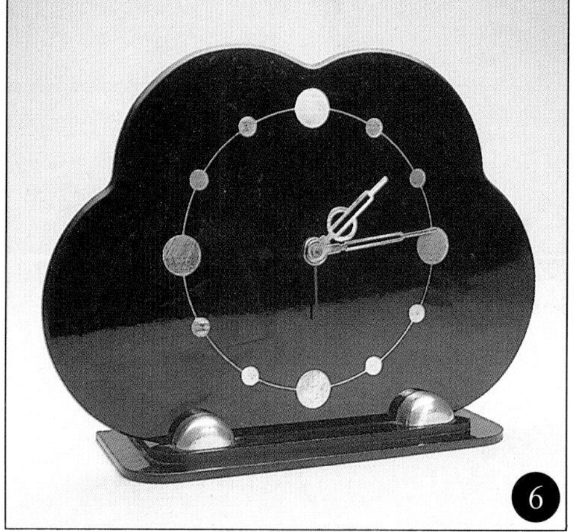

6 A flower-shaped clock made of Warerite, a hardened rubber. The legs, hands, and dial are aluminum. The clock was made in Britain. 1940s.

7 A clock with owl surround. Owls seem to have been quite a popular motif during the 1920s and 1930s, and this must be one of the finest examples. The body is made of two pieces with both legs screwed into it. Filled celluloid. 1920s.

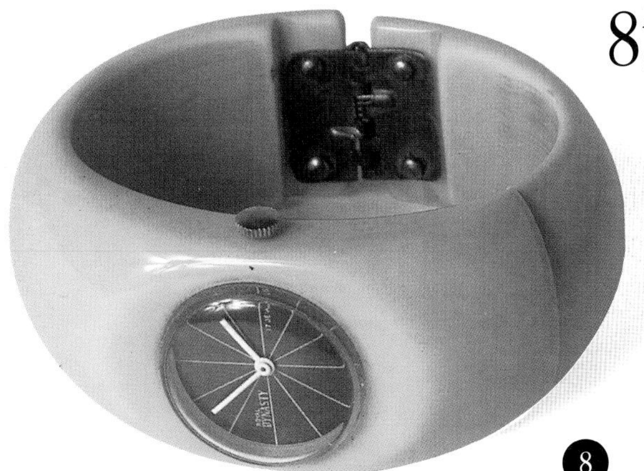

8 *Bakelite watch (it works!).*

9 *Clear cast phenolic watch pin.*

10 *Clock, by JAZ. Typical of French Art Deco style, the maroon and black case has chromium embellishments, and semicircular patterning is embossed within the stylized face. Cast phenolic and chromium. 1934.*

Art Deco

The Art Deco style, called the "Moderne" in America, introduced highly stylized abstract geometric forms derived from several sources. It had its roots in the revolutionary modern art movement of the Paris of the mid-twenties when rebellious artists were producing geometric patterns and forms in startling colors, thrusting aside the stylized natural forms and colors of earlier Art Nouveau. Into this melting pot of art went Machine Age concepts, Cubism (which had, in its turn, borrowed freely from primitive art), constructivism, functionalism, kitsch, and many other new ideas. Stepped architectural forms and motifs were drawn from preChristian cultures such as Aztec, Mayan, and Egyptian. Stylized floral patterns were derived from Japanese prints and textiles and also from the Viennese Arts and Crafts Movement of the late nineteenth century. Zigzags, lightning bolts, stylized fountains, and sunbursts alluded to the development of electricity and technological progress. The vivid color palette of Art Deco was inspired by Persian and Oriental examples. Manufacturers of plastic jewelry in particular, were seduced by the wealth of color and exotic motifs of Art Deco and even fine designers began to work in synthetic materials.

A pair of carved and cut-through bangles, one of many examples of Art Deco design.

Art Deco took its name from the Exposition Internationale des Arts Décoratifs et Industriels Modernes held in Paris in 1925. Although it was at first a luxury style that made use of materials like ivory, ebony, lacquer, and enamel, its popularity soon spread. Jazzy, modern—and relatively cheap—it appealed to people who were suffering the effects of the Depression at the end of the twenties. Art Deco is synonymous with many Hollywood films of the thirties and reached a vast public through this escapist medium. It is part of the architectural environment—William Van Alen's glittering Chrysler building is an Art Deco jewel on the Manhattan skyline. And its influence can be seen in innumerable Bakelite radios of the period. The style soon became mass-produced and was applied to a plethora of decorative objects and household items—cigarette cases, cocktail shakers, jewelry, and accessories—made from new materials like plastics.

The Favorite, by Elmi. This has to be one of the most decorative loudspeakers made, with a dove clasping an olive branch in a sky of geometric Art Deco squares. Bakelite. 1928.

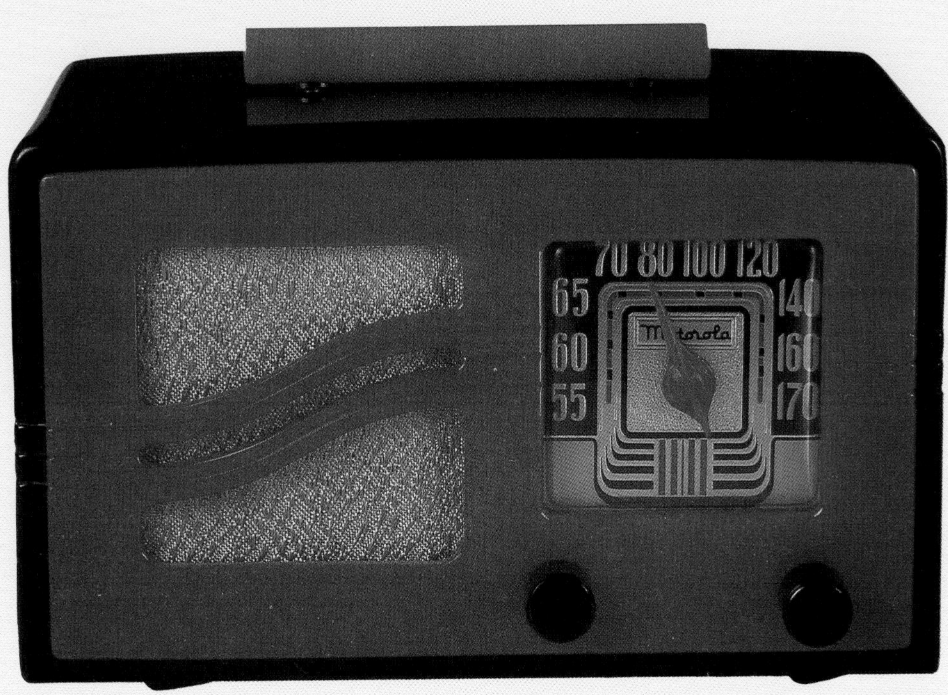

A striking Art Deco design that was the last of Motorola's classic Catalin radios.

Leisure and pleasure

In the thirties cast-phenolic resin was used for a multitude of purposes, from poker chips and chessmen to children's toys, dominoes, and mah-jong pieces to picnic sets and vacuum flasks. During this era, smoking was becoming increasingly popular, due to vigorous promotion by the major tobacco companies. The result was a profusion of Bakelite ashtrays and smoker's paraphernalia. Bakelite ashtrays came in all shapes and sizes, mostly black and brown, and often bearing commercial logos.

Black phenolic ashtrays were used on the luxury liner *Queen Mary* in 1934. A variety of sizes were designed to accommodate not only cigarettes and cigars, but also pipes. Occasionally ashtrays were disguised as decorative objects. "The Smoker's Friend" was a semicircular cigarette box with a swivel-out ashtray concealed inside. There was even a phenolic bedside smoker's kit featuring receptacles for cigarettes, matches, and ashtray in one molded object.

Smoking

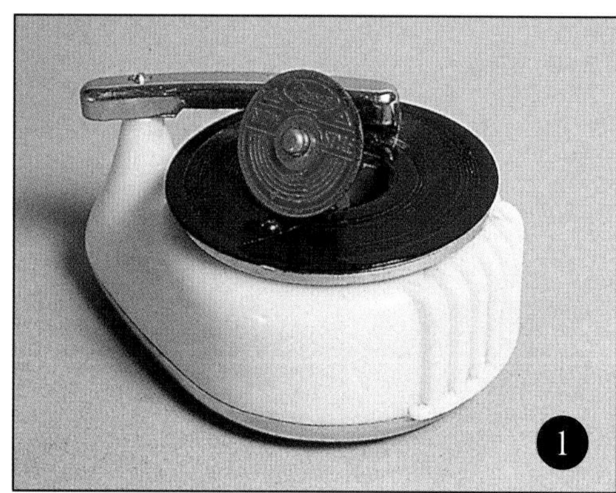

1 Cigarette lighter, by Prince. A really oddball idea this, a lighter in the shape of a record player. To ignite the flame, a knob is turned, causing the center of the record to pop up, which strikes a flint and … hey presto! Urea-formaldehyde and metal. 1948.

2 Cigarette case. This highly sought after cigarette case, made of multicolored celluloid, features a grasping hand that acts as a clasp to keep the case from opening. In addition, an inset compass points you in the direction of the nearest tobacconist! 1920s.

3 Match striker, by Alfred Dunhill. The ultimate in grotesque, a stumpy plump bird with an outrageous Mohican hairstyle! In fact this is only one of numerous creatures made as strikers by Dunhill in the 1930s. The body is cast-phenolic resin with an ebony beak, and the striking material is shark's skin. 1930s.

4 Michelin man ashtray. Was given away as a premium, this stylish ashtray has the curvaceous and full-bodied appearance characteristic of the 1940s. Available in black, brown, and green Bakelite with a urea-formaldehyde Michelin man. 1940s.

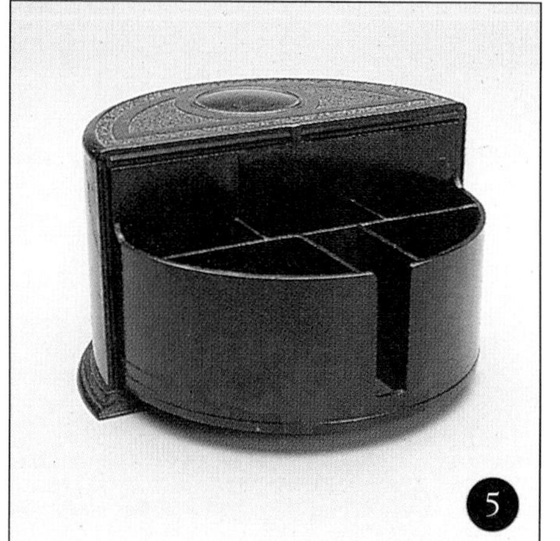

5 Linsden cigarette dispenser, a semicircular box of Edwardian style that opens out to a full circle to offer its contents. Bakelite. 1925.

6 Dunlop ashtrays, by Roanoid Ltd so named because they were used as a premium by them. An outstanding example of Art Deco design ingenuity, the ashtray's three arms may be closed to keep the ash inside, making it portable. It is also impossible, due to a lead weight at the center of its base, to turn the ashtray over. Made in five different colors of thiourea-formaldehyde with black Bakelite bases. 1930s.

7 Bakelite cigarette holder with original case.

For children

1 Codeg car. More obviously a toy than the Golden Arrow, being pulled by a string fed through the front bumper, the Codeg car is nonetheless an exceptionally beautiful piece of Art Deco sculpture in plastic. Luxuriously curved and streamlined, the car bears a strong resemblance to the contemporary Cord sports car. Available in various colors, Bakelite body, celluloid windscreen. Late 1940s.

2 Golden Arrow record car, by Automobiles Geographical Ltd. Certainly the finest Bakelite car model and one of the most sensational of all Bakelite objects, the Golden Arrow replicates the eponymous winner of the 1929 land speed record, which was designed by Sir Henry Segrave. It is incredible to believe now that this prized piece was actually a toy; indeed, with its clockwork motor and adjustable steering, the full-sized version would have played havoc in any child's playroom. Very rare, especially in complete working order. 1929.

3 Locomotive and wagons, by E. Eliot Ltd. In the same league as the Codeg car, this train is a high quality toy and eminently collectible. The simplification of form and the angular streamlining owes much to the influence of Henry Dreyfuss. Phenolic. 1940s.

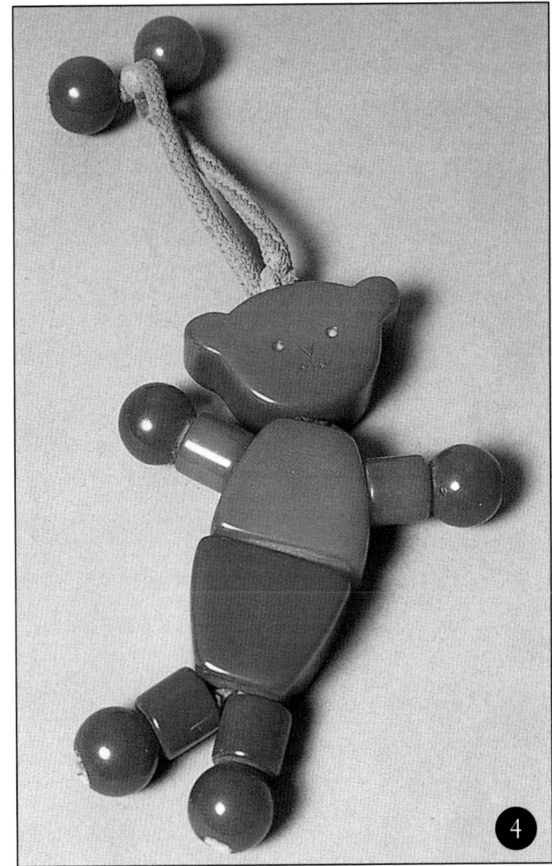

4 Crib toy. Cast phenolic crib toys were popular in America in the 1930s and can be found in various animal and human forms, this one being in the shape of a teddy bear. Cast phenolic was a clear improvement on celluloid as a material for children's toys, being so much stronger.

5 *Eagle children's projector, by Martin Lucas Ltd. An amusing example of the most static of objects being given the airflow styling treatment so redundant in strictly functional terms, if not in aesthetic ones. Bakelite. 1938.*

6 *Money box. Perhaps to intimidate would-be thieves, this exact miniature of a traditional British police phone box is in fact a child's savings box. Bakelite. 1930s.*

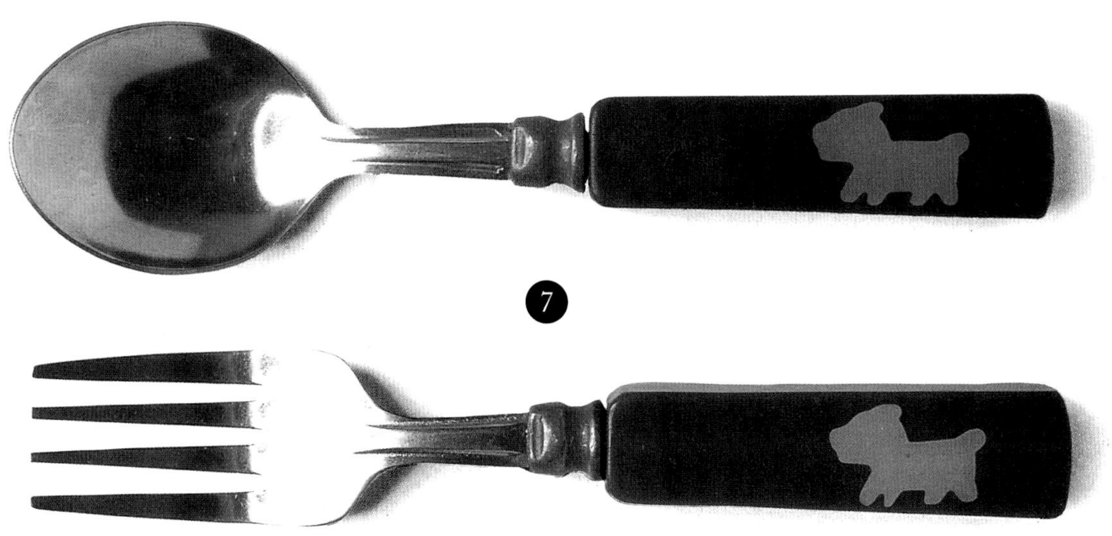

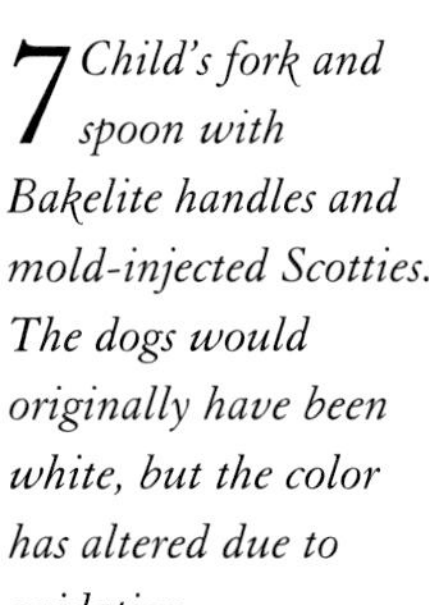

7 *Child's fork and spoon with Bakelite handles and mold-injected Scotties. The dogs would originally have been white, but the color has altered due to oxidation.*

Cocktails

1 The Master Incolor Cocktail Shaker, molded for William & Gill, by Thomas de la Rue. A magnificent cocktail shaker whose cap rotates to reveal numerous recipes: the Bronx, Clover Club, Dry Martini, Tom Collins, Manhattan, Orange Blossom, Sidecar, and Whisky Sour can all be found on its recipe ring. The shaker also has a large strainer "for perfect mixing" and a "magicork spout that ensures no spillage." It came in a range of six stylish colors, all with silverplated measuring caps. Urea-formaldehyde. c, 1935.

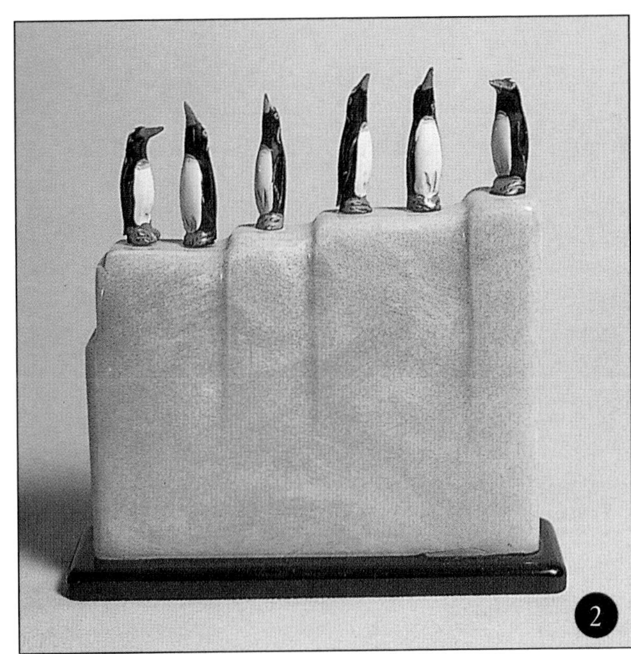

2 Cocktail sticks. A humorous set of six penguin-crowned silver cocktail sticks all sitting happily on a yellow iceberg. Yellow iceberg? It seems quite plausible to assume that it was, in fact, once white and has simply reacted to the sun's ultraviolet rays. Cast phenolic and silver. 1930s.

Picnic ware

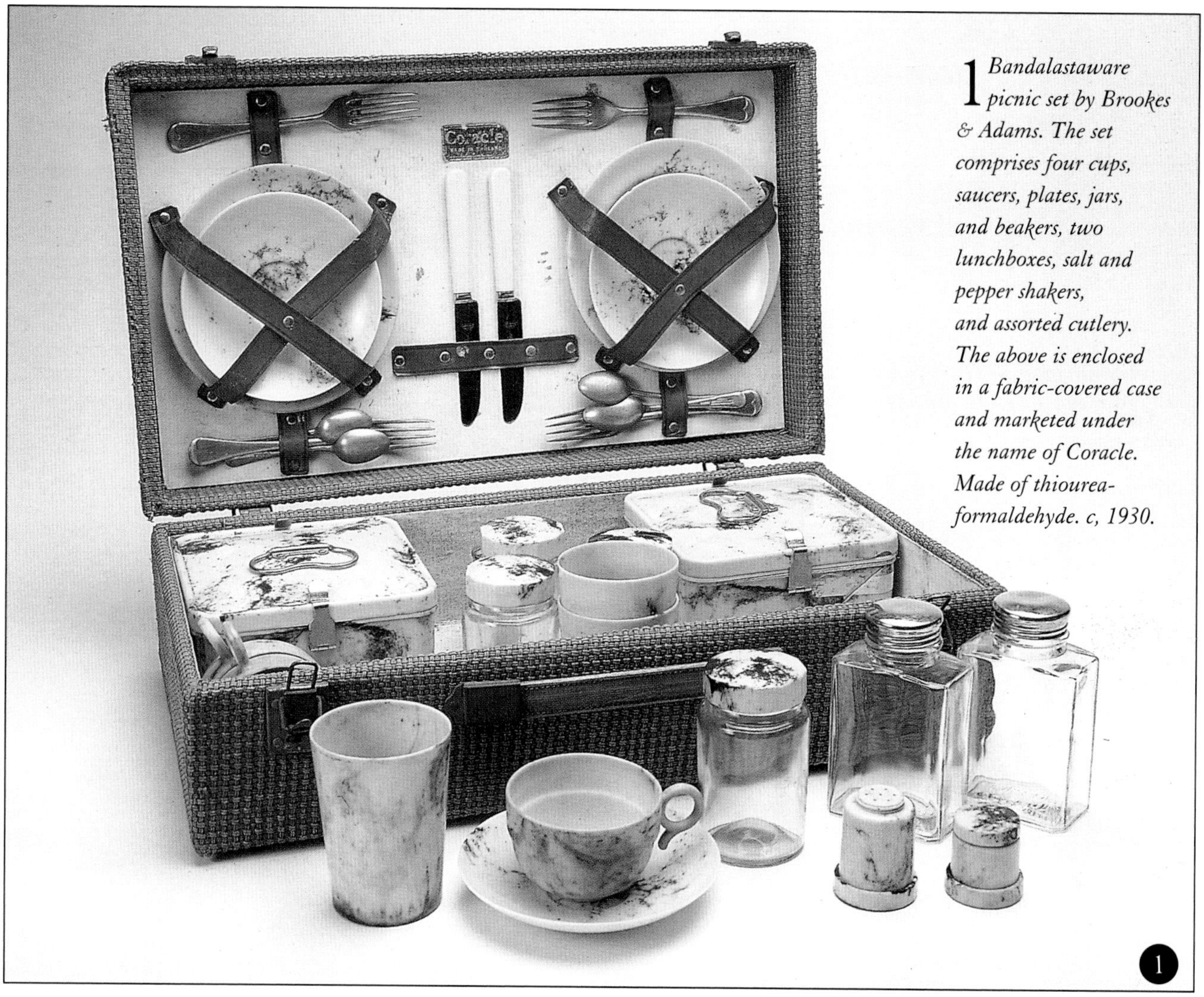

1 Bandalastaware picnic set by Brookes & Adams. The set comprises four cups, saucers, plates, jars, and beakers, two lunchboxes, salt and pepper shakers, and assorted cutlery. The above is enclosed in a fabric-covered case and marketed under the name of Coracle. Made of thiourea-formaldehyde. c, 1930.

2 Vacuum jug, by the British Vacuum Flask Co. With its distinctive molded decoration, this item was marketed as a multifunctional flask, not to be used merely at picnics. Urea-formaldehyde. 1940s.

3 Vacuum flask, by Thermos. A really striking oblong flask solely designed to fit snugly into large Bandalasta picnic sets. Made in blue, alabaster, or green thiorea-formaldehyde. Late 1940s.

4 *Vacuum flask, by Thermos 1925 Ltd. The classic Thermos, of fluted Art Nouveau style, was available in a range of different urea-formaldehyde colors. 1930.*

5 *Vacuum flask, by Thermos 1925 Ltd. These curvaceous jugs, reminiscent of futuristic penguins, were made from thiorea-formaldehyde. 1940s.*

6 *Thermos vacuum flask. Its bloated appearance was a typical feature of 1940s design. Urea-formaldehyde with acrylic handle and stopper. 1940s.*

Games and gambling

1 *Metal Klikatelle, bagatelle board and domino gaming machine—both from the Prohibition era. Bakelite. 1930s.*

2 *Butler gaming chips, made in different colors of casein, and multicolored Halma gaming pegs made out of urea-formaldehyde. Probably 1930s.*

3 Table tennis bats. Very stylish and unusual Bakelite bats with celluloid ping-pong ball. 1930s.

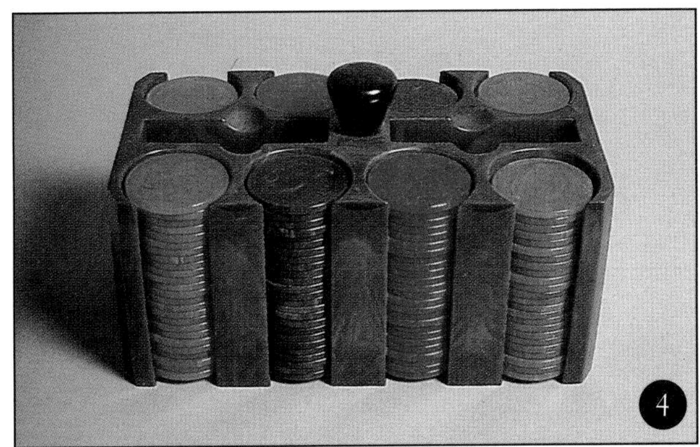

4 Poker chip set. During the 1930s and 1940s a wide variety of gaming and gaming-related items were made. Many, like this impressive poker set, feature beautiful combinations of luxurious marbling effects and rich colors. Cast phenolic. 1940s.

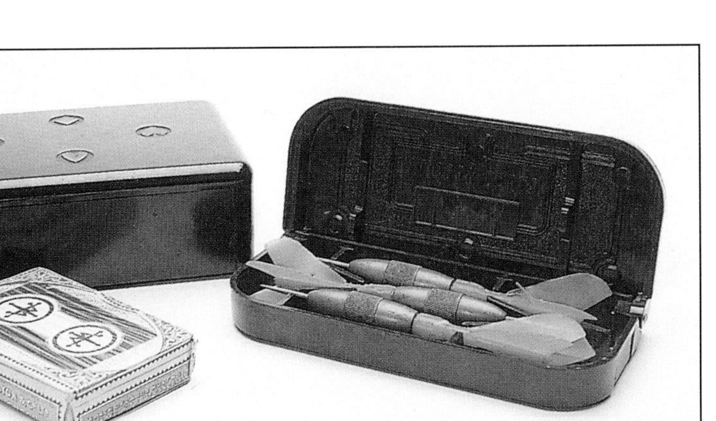

5 Unicorn darts in Bakelite box. Three brass darts with polythene feathers and a Bakelite card box with a molded lid.

6 Chess set. A large and magnificent traditional chess set in black and butterscotch carved cast phenolic. Although the maker is unknown, this would certainly have been a deluxe and expensive set. 1930s.

Photography

The art of photography owes much to the invention of plastics. The earliest cameras were based on the principle of a solid metal or glass plate coated with a light-sensitive emulsion of silver nitrate. This gave rise to the first generation of cameras which were large, bulky objects mounted on tripods. The notion of replacing the rigid support with a flexible film first occurred in the late 1880s. A New Jersey pastor, Hannibal Goodwin, discovered how to make celluloid (the first commercially successful plastic developed by the Hyatt brothers) into a thin, transparent film. Henry Reichenback, a chemist working for George Eastman's photographic supply house in Rochester, New York, made a similar discovery and devised a method of producing photographic film from celluloid. From its introduction in 1889, celluloid film had a profound impact on the evolution of photography and was subsequently used by Thomas Edison in his experiments to develop the cine-camera. The success of early motion pictures was marred only by the intense flammability of the film itself, which was the cause of many fires in projection rooms. By the 1920s, the outcome of persistent research resulted in cellulose acetate replacing celluloid as an alternative, nonflammable film base.

As interest in photography spread, the demand for less cumbersome equipment grew. In response to this new market, dozens of companies in Europe and America began to produce cheap, basic cameras molded in sturdy, durable phenolic resin. In America these sold for as little as 49 cents up to a couple of dollars. Most worked on the basic "point and shoot" principle which required no focusing and represented little improvement on the first portable Brownie camera introduced by George Eastman's Kodak company in 1900, which retailed at one dollar. But for Kodak, the undisputed leader in the field, and for other manufacturers, simplicity spelled profit. Kodak's 1934 "Baby Brownie," with its case—a black phenolic box with a distinctive vertical ribbing—designed by Walter Dorwin Teague, reportedly sold four million at a dollar apiece. Bakelite proved ideally suited to the demands of mass production and from the 1930s onwards was used to manufacture box cameras in an immense variety of models and sizes. Kodak made extensive use of mottled Bakelite in its early "Hawkette" range of cameras, which incorporated a miniature foldout bellows and were available only by mail order during the twenties.

In general, early camera designs, such as the "Rodenstock" of 1935, tended to be phenolic imitations of metal boxes covered in Leatherette—even down to the sharp corners—but designs began to emerge that were better suited to the characteristics of new materials. The Agfa "Trolix" of 1936 incorporated curved sides, rounded corners, decorative ribs and a shiny surface—all typical of thirties' streamlining, but such features would have been very difficult to realize in metal. One outstanding design of the period is the 1937 "Purma," conceived by the American industrial designer Raymond Loewy. This integral unit took the form of an elegantly tapered rectangular case of Bakelite, finely grooved for a firm grip. Unlike most other models, the wind-on mechanism, shutter speed indicator and button switch did not protrude from the body, giving the impression of a neat and smoothly functional camera. The Purma Special also offered the intriguing innovations of a Perspex viewfinder and three-speed focal plane shutter that worked by gravity, according to the position in which the camera was held.

Many other types of camera were manufactured in Bakelite, including models such as the Corvette "Midget," a cheap, miniature camera sold in a variety of colors. Its sister model, the "Coronet," displays a typically streamlined form in which all the metal parts are countersunk and the surface texture is a phenolic imitation of Leatherette-covered metal. Bakelite box cameras continued to be produced until the mid-fifties, when manufacturers such as Kodak began to use lighter and less brittle plastics, which necessitated a different approach to design.

Unlike radios, which were constantly on view in the home, cameras tended to be packed away when not in use. This must, to some extent, account for the comparative lack of emphasis on styling and limited number of design variations, but Bakelite cameras of the thirties and forties remain eminently collectible, despite these aesthetic shortcomings.

Brownie 127 camera, by Kodak. First introduced in 1952, the Brownie went through only minor changes in design right up until 1963. Its body is ridged with horizontal indented lines and the lens is surrounded by a crosshatched decorative aluminum plate. Kodak tried only once to change their market leader: they produced a white version that got so grubby that nobody wanted to use it! Black polystyrene, urea-formaldehyde knobs. 1956.

Cameras

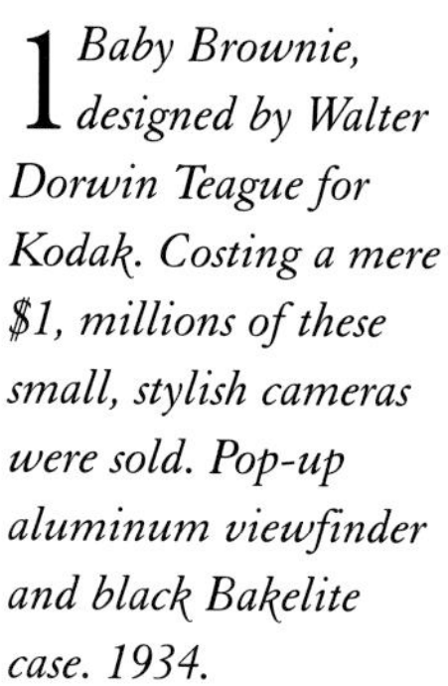

1 *Baby Brownie, designed by Walter Dorwin Teague for Kodak. Costing a mere $1, millions of these small, stylish cameras were sold. Pop-up aluminum viewfinder and black Bakelite case. 1934.*

2 *Coronet Midget, by Coronet Camera Co. At the time the smallest camera ever made, the Coronet took a 16mm film, and was produced in a multitude of eye-catching mottled and solid colors, blue certainly being the rarest and most desirable. Bakelite. 1937.*

3 Pic camera model 870468. This camera is not only a charming echo of the circular Ekco and RCA radios; it is also reminiscent of the Tikka spy camera, which is disguised as a pocket-watch. The shape is practical and will slip into a top pocket with ease. Styrene. Late 1940s.

4 *Hawkette, by Kodak. In the 1930s, in response to the growing number of amateur photographers, dozens of companies in the USA and abroad began to produce cheap basic cameras molded in sturdy Bakelite. This British example is one of the very earliest and was given away as a premium with such diverse products as Cadbury's chocolates and Australian cigarettes. 1927.*

5 *Purma Special, designed by Raymond Loewy. A beautifully designed and innovative camera, the Purma Special incorporated a plastic viewfinder system and a unique wind-on mechanism, encased in a compact body. Its dimensions and shape blazed a trail for 1930s camera design. 1937.*

Projectors

1 Filmosto's Filmstar slide projector. In this startling departure from the traditional boxy shape, the converging lines of the barrel serve to stress the direction of the light beam—as if it were a ray gun! Bakelite. 1952.

2 Magnajector, by Peter Austin Manufacturing Co. The Magnajector operates through a series of angled mirrors and lenses to lift, magnify and project two-dimensional images such as text or photographs placed beneath it. Bakelite. Late 1930s.

3 Dux Episcop. Similar in function to the Magnajector although a very clumsy design, it is partly saved by the bold logo panel on the side. Bakelite. 1951.

Television

With the advent of television in the late forties, another new and receptive market opened up for Bakelite. "It is natural that designers who have already proved the worth of molded radio cabinets should employ Bakelite materials in the television field," proclaimed a 1950 edition of *Bakelite Progress*, the magazine produced by the marketing department of Bakelite Limited. Like radios, Bakelite television cabinets were free from the design limitations and complex manufacturing processes imposed by natural materials and these advantages were seized upon as a marketing tool. A 1949 article in *Modern Plastics* considered the number of operations in the manufacture of a wood and a molded phenolic television cabinet—the wooden cabinet required some 500 separate actions before the television chassis could be inserted, compared to only half a dozen for its phenolic counterpart.

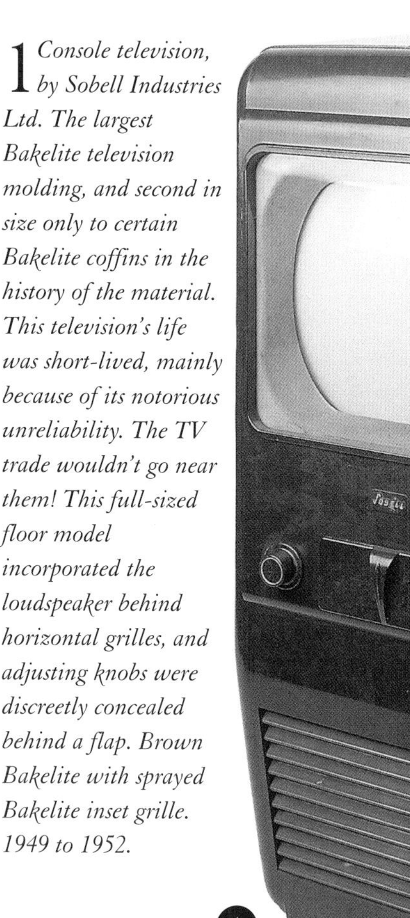

1 Console television, by Sobell Industries Ltd. The largest Bakelite television molding, and second in size only to certain Bakelite coffins in the history of the material. This television's life was short-lived, mainly because of its notorious unreliability. The TV trade wouldn't go near them! This full-sized floor model incorporated the loudspeaker behind horizontal grilles, and adjusting knobs were discreetly concealed behind a flap. Brown Bakelite with sprayed Bakelite inset grille. 1949 to 1952.

Molded phenolic cabinets did indeed offer important advantages—ease of handling on the production line and the elimination of difficult and costly machining operations. The finished article emerged from the press complete with strengthening ribs, loudspeaker grille, and metal inserts, all of which were incorporated during the molding process. Such techniques were similar to those used in the manufacture of radios, but the molds for one-piece television cabinets were necessarily larger, with a consequent increase in the size and capacity of the molding apparatus. To produce a modestly proportioned, three-foot-high television cabinet with a ten-inch screen, the American Admiral Corporation used a giant 30ft-high molding press capable of delivering 2,000 tons of pressure to each individual molding. The production cycle lasted seven minutes

2 Bush TV 12. Certainly the most well known and most desired of all British Bakelite televisions. Early television technology employed a system of 405 lines to a screen, and when 625 lines came along in 1964 these televisions became obsolete. Horrendous rumors circulate that many TV 12s and a similar model, the TV 22, were shipped to Japan and turned into fish tanks! Bakelite. 1949.

and could be repeated several times a day. Mass production on this scale inevitably helped to bring retail prices down. Admiral Corporation's television sold for just under $12.50 in 1949.

These production methods were also used in the creation of one-piece molded phenolic cabinets for phonographs marketed by Admiral, Philips, and others. Many of these were portable, such as the rare late twenties' 12-inch Philips player, which packed up into a circular Bakelite case resembling a hatbox. By the mid-fifties, however, both television and radio technology had made substantial advances, with miniaturized electronic components replacing their bulky predecessors. This served radically to alter the design of the finished product, as postwar designers began to place less emphasis on streamlining and curvaceous styling. The bold, flowing lines of thirties and forties Bakelite gradually gave way to a spare and ascetic vision, which ushered in a new era of industrial design.

3 Philips portable phonograph Type 3902. Unusual in as much as the player and its mechanism are totally encased in a Bakelite housing. Early 1950s.

Functionalism

The basic principles of form, function, and space formed the basis of Functionalist doctrine and were put into practice by the influential Bauhaus school of architecture and design. Established in Weimar, Germany, in 1919, under the direction of Walter Gropius, it produced a number of influential architects and designers, notably Le Corbusier. It concentrated on a combination of craftsmanship with mechanization and its style was characterized by severely geometric forms. Design took into account the nature of the materials that were used.

Among the Bauhaus's many ambitious aims was to create a number of prototype household objects suitable for mass production, thus bringing modern design within easier reach of the public. Despite, or perhaps because of, its radical reputation, the ideals of the Bauhaus were not shared by the ruling Nazi party, which conspired to close the school in 1933. As a consequence, many of the Bauhaus's most prominent teachers emigrated to the United States. The few prototypes that were produced during the school's short lifetime—such as Marcel Breuer's austere tubular steel furniture—are now regarded as classics of modern design.

In Britain, in 1934, the architect Wells Coates designed the famous circular AD65 for Ekco. Coates' training—he had worked with Le Corbusier and also designed the Lawn Road apartments in Hampstead in north London in 1933—is clearly reflected in the design of the AD65.

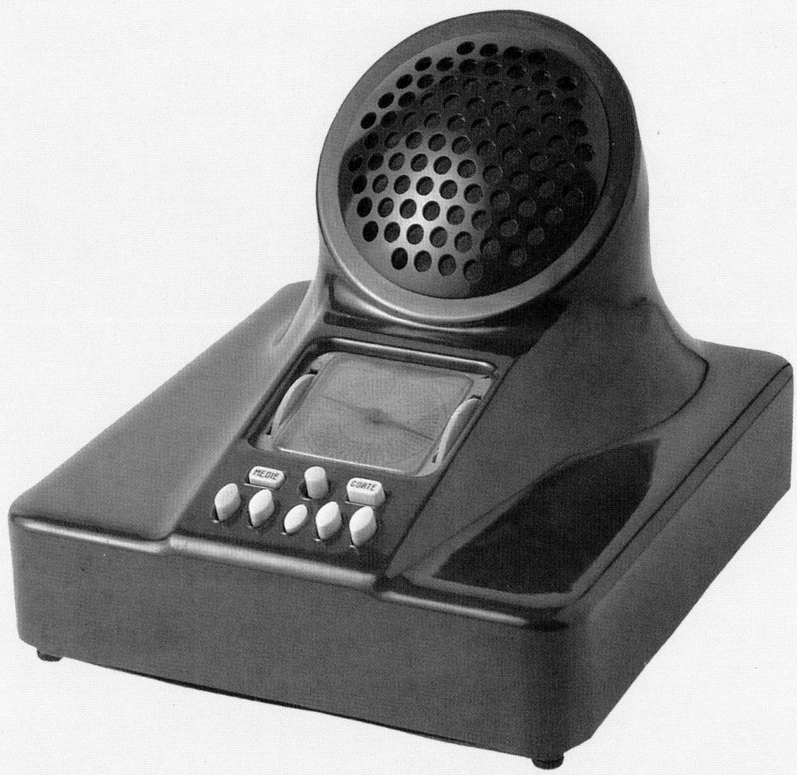

Designed by Castiglioni, this Phonola of 1939 is the only radio to be exhibited in New York's Museum of Modern Art. Artfully playing with the ideas of form and function, the radio is meant to resemble a telephone so that the public would recognize it as a piece of modern equipment.

Bakelite really did release the designer's hand. For the first time in Britain an architect, Wells Coates, revolutionized the design of the radio with his Ekco model AD65 of 1934. Known as the "Round Ekco," it was the first of five very successful models produced in either "walnut" or black Bakelite with chrome-plated trim. Non-standard colors such as a marbleized green version were available to special order.

Radios

A remarkable variety of Bakelite radios was produced in many countries from the mid-twenties until a few years after World War II. They range from the early, stylish but restrained Art Deco designs to the extravagant and even outrageous objects that marked the sad but triumphant end of the golden age of radio.

It was the introduction of plastics, beginning with Bakelite, which freed cabinet designers from the constraints that had been imposed on their creative endeavors by the necessity of employing the traditional natural materials—mainly wood—which produced furniture-style cabinets intended to blend with the interior accouterments of the typical home of the thirties. New design movements like that of the Bauhaus, as well as influences from modern art, were changing architecture and interiors which now needed equipment to match. Innovative designers began to produce furniture in the new style, which meant that the old wooden-box radio became an anachronism in fashionable homes. The immense design possibilities of plastics as well as their ability to match mass-production requirements was rapidly to change the look of the radio. At first, the new avant-garde designs appealed only to well-to-do, style-conscious people but were resisted by ordinary homemakers who could not afford to change everything instantly to keep up with the whims of the stylists; for them, the Art Deco Bakelite radio would have been an impudent anachronism in the living-room. Consequently, the more extreme upmarket designs were diluted for the mass-market until general furnishing style came up to date, to the chagrin of designers who saw the innovative shapes and bright colors of their creations debased into more traditional styles which imitated dark-brown wood. But for many reasons, particularly the increasing cost of rare woods from the already plundered and depleted rain forests, plastics were here to stay. Radios were to become part of the Machine Age and their form reflected the spirit of the age, symbolizing the middle of a Depression, the jazzy lifestyles of high society, and the exciting promise of automated technology to free working people from drudgery and unemployment. Radios took the forms of the monolithic, soaring skyscraper; the streamlined airplane; the thundering locomotive and the kitsch automobile, reflecting all of the vibrant forms and colors of modern art.

These developments began as small movements but rapidly spread all over the world. The examples that follow are from the United States, Britain, France, Germany, Italy, Spain, Czechoslovakia, and Australia—all of which stamped an individuality on their designs.

The evolution of the radio cabinet

The world's first radio broadcast took place in the Netherlands in 1919. This was followed by broadcasts in the USA a year later and in Britain and Germany in 1922. The advent and spread of public service broadcasting in Europe and America brought with it a great increase in the demand for radios. Between 1920 and 1927 annual sales of radio receivers in the USA rose from $2 million to $136 million, a reflection of the growth in the number of American radio stations from three to 800 over the same period. By 1931 radio as a public service broadcasting medium had spread all over the world and America was launching radio's golden age.

In embryo form, in the mid-twenties, the early radio had consisted of a wooden board on which were mounted a few components like coils, glass bulbs, rotary-vane condensers, dials, and tuning knobs. It was all connected together by a spider's web of wires and attached to a pack of large batteries, a pair of earphones or a loudspeaker. Requiring even more wire to provide an aerial and ground, this ugly assembly seemed chaotic, but made sense electronically, so the components could not be easily changed or repositioned simply to please the eye of the cosmeticist.

However, most of the components could be put into a box and, by then, a loudspeaker had been devised. This was achieved simply by adding a gramophone horn to the earphone which had been used for personal listening. Later, flat "cone" loudspeakers in square wooden boxes replaced decorated freestanding horns. To get enough volume to drive increasingly larger loudspeakers, an amplifier was added. This used power-hungry tubes to make sounds louder—and these in turn demanded large, heavy and expensive batteries to run, since few people then had domestic electric power. Radios were therefore beginning to become quite large and more complicated, so that they could not be easily disguised or hidden away. As a result, designers made

1

1 Philips model 634A. It is known affectionately as the "Ovaltiney Set" after its appearance in a British television commercial in the early 1980s. With its Bakelite loudspeaker and dial surround, it is an excellent example of a decorative marriage between Bakelite and wood.

them part of the acceptable furniture of the living-room, constructing them as cupboards, chests on legs, dressers, writing-boxes, and desks.

This approach changed abruptly, when a craftsman had the idea of putting all the electronic components of the radio, including the batteries and an aerial wound on a frame, into a square wooden box, then cutting a round hole in the front for the loudspeaker, creating the first entirely self-contained cabinet radio. Next, the speaker aperture was covered with decorative silk cloth and framed with fretwork ornamental grilles of fancy woods and metals. At first, these were in Art Nouveau patterns of interwoven natural forms and later of designs derived from recently discovered Egyptian tomb and Mayan temple art forms which pointed the way to an Art Deco style.

The real radio cabinet had arrived!

3 Goltone Super crystal set. This was probably the first-ever Bakelite receiver. 1925.

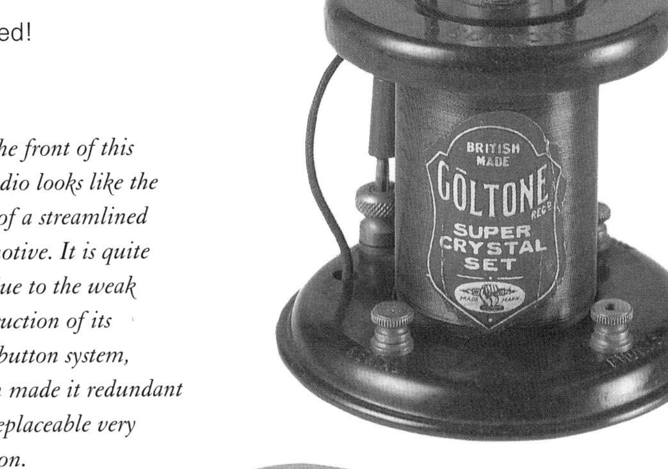

2 The front of this radio looks like the front of a streamlined locomotive. It is quite rare due to the weak construction of its push-button system, which made it redundant and replaceable very early on.

4 This miniature portable, manufactured in Perspex by Pye as the model M78F, was ill-fated. Resembling almost exactly the Japanese flag, the symbol of Britain's former enemy, it was withdrawn, resulting today in a much-desired and rare set.

5 British Thomson Houston Co. Ltd. A very popular loudspeaker of which over a million were sold between 1923 and 1930 for the princely sum of £5 5s (approximately $7.50). Bakelite and aluminum. 1923.

6 Philips speakers Type 2003. The larger of the two speakers measures 19 inches in diameter, representing the biggest molding to be produced up to that time. Manufactured in many striking swirled colors, it was designed specifically as an objet d'art to enhance its marketability. Bakelite. 1927.

7 Philips' Stars and Stripes. This loudspeaker sports the Philips logo and looks very much like the Philips 930A radio of the same year. Bakelite. 1931.

Bakelite cabinets

It was the late twenties before Bakelite was first used for moldings as large as radio cabinets, although its suitability for mass-producing a huge variety of small objects from toys and telephones to Ford car gearwheels was seen from the very beginning. The reasons were twofold. Firstly, the capital costs of installing the gigantic presses and of making the large press-tools needed for Bakelite moldings were not within the means of the industry until it coalesced at around 1930 from a myriad small firms into a group of very large and profitable ones. The second reason was resistance from potential customers to brighter colors and new shapes. They had been accustomed from the beginning of radio production to buying radios which matched the hand-me-down Victorian furniture in their stuffy parlors—cabinets made from "real" wood that looked like furniture.

To counter the resistance, Bakelite dyes were used to provide mottled effects in brown Bakelite which gave a fair simulation of wood finishes; but potential customers were not really fooled. They wanted the cosy "warmth" and attractive "graining" that was unique to each individual real-wood cabinet, and claimed with some justification that natural wood made the radio sound better. Despite these objections Bakelite soon became popular among less wealthy customers who were prepared to put up with these radios because they were cheaper. Even so, there continued to be a certain amount of resistance to Bakelite radio cabinets, which had in some quarters acquired the "cheap and nasty" image. This unfair reputation had been earned by the inappropriate use of previous plastics as substitutes for natural materials in cheap, badly designed products some years earlier. In the case of radios, Bakelite was seen as a substitute for the "real thing," precisely because it was often used to imitate wood, and it was some years before it came into its own as a material for radios like the one illustrated here.

The GEC model BC 4941, by General Electric Co, dates from 1948 and is an early portable battery radio, which resembles a bowling bag in terms of both appearance and weight. So much for portable! It was made in a variety of colored Bakelites.

The United States

1 *The Air King designed by Harold Van Doren. It was the first American radio to be truly different from its wooden precursors. To that date, it was the largest American plastic molding. The stepped-skyscraper design, waterfall façade, and engraved plaque depicting a map of the world are surely the most spectacular features to be found on any radio. Made of Plaskon (US trade name for urea-formaldehyde) in various colors. 1933.*

American radio manufacturers were slow to seize the potential of new plastic materials like Bakelite. It was not until the Depression of the early thirties, and the increased popularity of radio broadcasting, that the emergent American plastics industry was provided with the optimum conditions for cornering a significant proportion of the market. By 1938, out of a total of six million radio sets sold, around 1.5 million were made of some form of plastic, reflecting the output of dozens of companies and a staggering variety of designs. Initially, American radio designers, like their counterparts elsewhere, attempted to imitate the ornate "Gothic cathedral" style of old wooden cabinets, but details such as pointed arches and elaborate relief patterns proved incompatible with the new plastic molding techniques, which favored rounded edges, plain, unadorned surfaces, and a horizontal rather than vertical format. It took some time for the public to accept these modern design features and a strange, new material, but in 1936 the prestigious Sears department store gave modernity and plastics its official stamp of approval, with the introduction of the "Silvertone" compact radio, designed by John Morgan. Retailing at $12.50, the Silvertone had a brown molded phenolic casing and an unusual wraparound grille, which gave the set a finished look.

Like the Silvertone, most American radios of the thirties were molded from Bakelite or other proprietary phenolic resins in either brown or black with contrasting grille cloths, knobs or dials in light-colored urea-formaldehyde. As the decade progressed, the fashion for lighter colors increased and radios were produced in white- or cream-colored urea moldings or in darker phenolic resins sprayed white. The new techniques of mass production greatly helped to lower the cost of the finished item. Engineers developed methods of making minor changes in the steel molds, so that models could be varied from year to year without destroying the costly original mold after only a single production run. A molded phenolic radio in dark-colored resin could be obtained for about $10 or less, but cast-phenolic sets were slightly more expensive, rarely selling for under $15. This was due to the casting process, which was more labor intensive and had a lower yield than high-pressure molding.

Cast-phenolic sets were formed by pouring the viscous phenolic syrup into lead molds. The castings were then placed in ovens to bake for around three days. Once removed from the molds as rough castings, they were hand polished and finished. The color of cast-phenolic resin tends to be richer and more intense than the molded material and radios made from cast phenolic retain their glowing color over the years, which makes them extremely popular with collectors.

2 Colonial (New World) Globe, by the Colonial Radio Corporation. This "world" radio wasn't a universally popular best seller but, probably for this reason, is highly collectible today. The loudspeaker is lodged within the pyramid base, and the stations are tuned with the equatorial knobs. Upon the globe's surface is a gold-embossed map of the world. Bakelite. 1933.

3 RCA model RC350. A midget in the true sense of the world, it measured a mere 7 x $4\frac{3}{4}$ x $4\frac{1}{4}$ inches! Especially attractive in this rare marbleized green version, its front grille area with its cut-out tulip design is unusual.

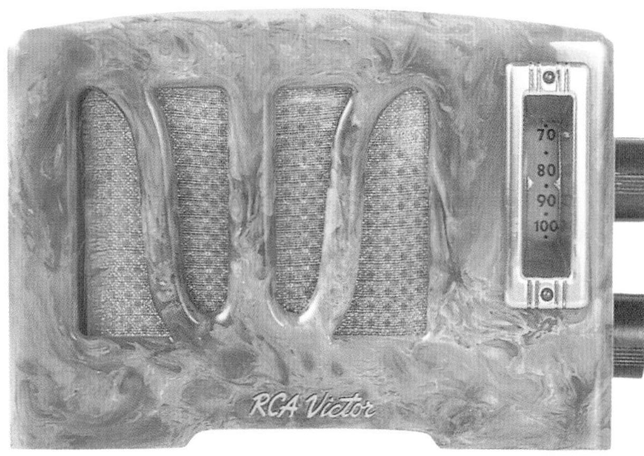

4 Kadette Jewel. This aptly named midget radio with its contrasting marbleized fretwork grille and brass escutcheoned knobs is a sensational example of ornate Art Deco style. Mid-1930s.

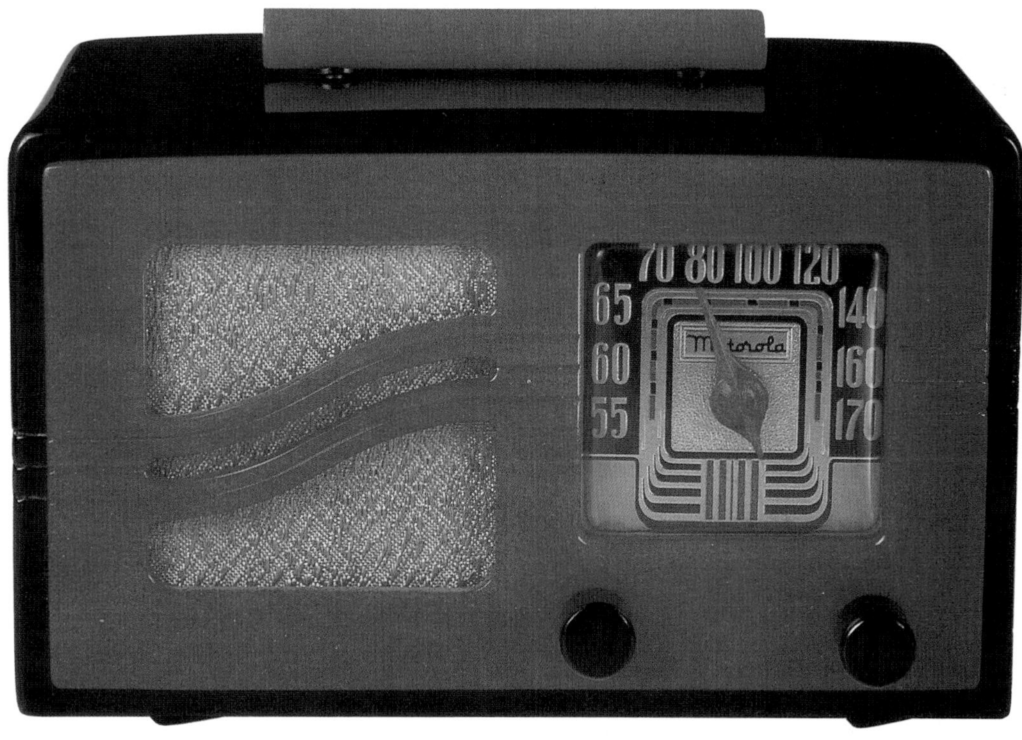

5 Motorola radio. A delightfully solid and striking Art Deco design with a sleek, S-shaped front panel and striking dial-face. This was the last of Motorola's classic Catalin models.

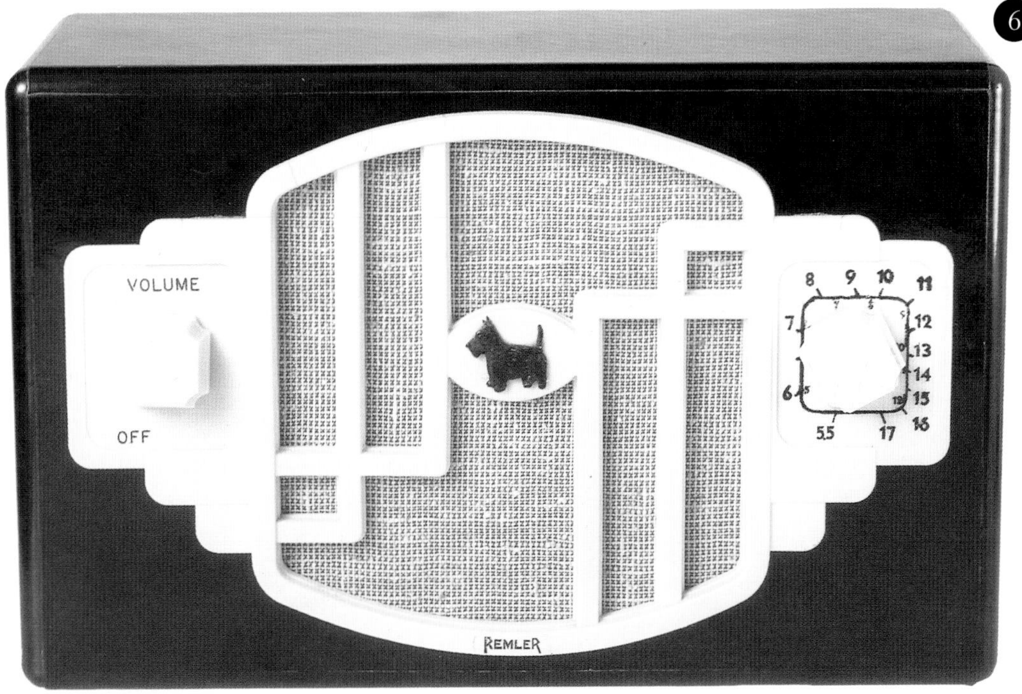

6 An unusual radio by Remler of Los Angeles, with a Roosevelt-inspired Scottie dog motif and geometric Art Deco design. It was one of many similar radios manufactured by the company in 1936.

7 Tombstone model AU 190, by Emerson. Despite its name it is a midget radio only 10 inches in height. Its early Gothic look harks back to its wooden ancestors and it is now highly prized in any of its dramatically marbleized colors. Catalin. 1937.

8 *Tombstone model U5A, by Emerson. This was a cheaper alternative to its internally identical, luxuriously marbleized Catalin cousin, the Emerson AU190. It was manufactured from Bakelite or Plaskon.*

9 *The Kadette Clockette. It was produced in a range of five stunning, luminescent Crystlin colors, the translucent glass-look blue being both the scarcest and most attractive. 1937.*

10 *Jewel Box, by General Electric. This aptly named radio, with its lavishly generous, thick, marbleized, sometimes translucent red case, and bulbous yellow knob is a joy to look at and touch.*

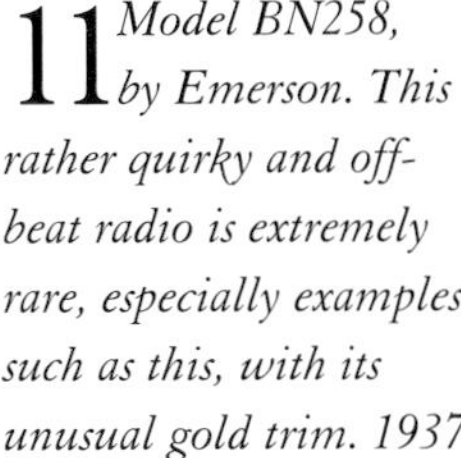

11 *Model BN258, by Emerson. This rather quirky and off-beat radio is extremely rare, especially examples such as this, with its unusual gold trim. 1937.*

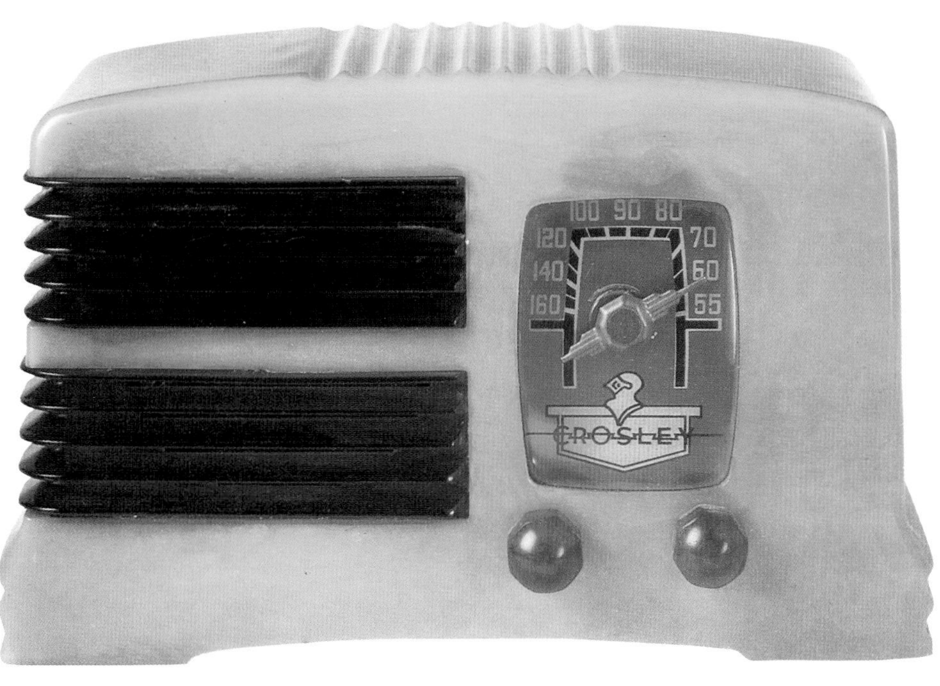

12 *A split grille, deeply grooved, knight-bedecked beauty produced by Crosley. Manufactured both in the United States and Canada it is considered rare in any of its three color combinations. 1938.*

13 *Wavemagnet, by Zenith. Although the company was a major player in the production of radios, it never moved very deeply into Bakelite cabinet production. This is probably its best, with its curvaceous, streamlined design, Art Deco dial, and incredible jutting out tuning knob. 1938.*

14 *Little Miracle model AX235, by Emerson. Available in a vast combination of grille and body colors, this charming midget radio of early design has been nicknamed the "Baby Emerson." The grille bows inwards on this model as a result of both heat and shrinkage. Catalin. 1938.*

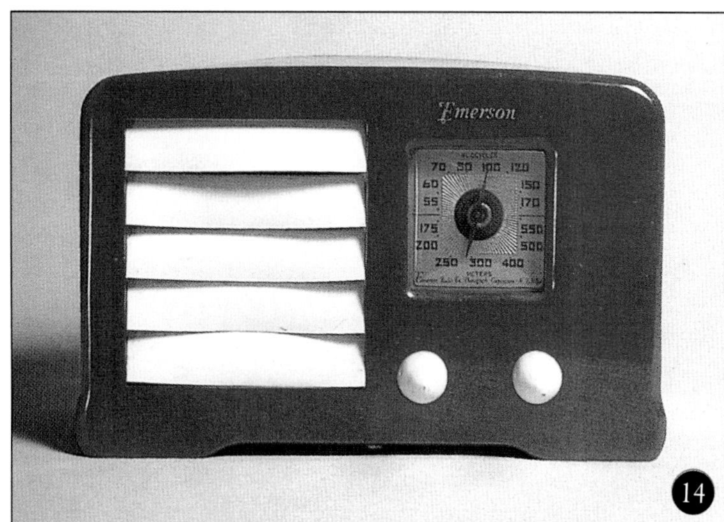

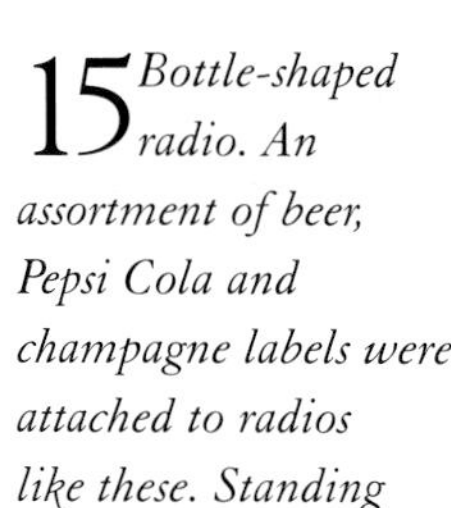

15 *Bottle-shaped radio. An assortment of beer, Pepsi Cola and champagne labels were attached to radios like these. Standing 3 feet tall, the bottle stopper acted as the tuning mechanism while the speaker was mounted upside down at its base. Bakelite.*

16 Detrola Super Pee Wee. This extremely small midget radio is rare in its blue-veined, Plaskon form. 1938.

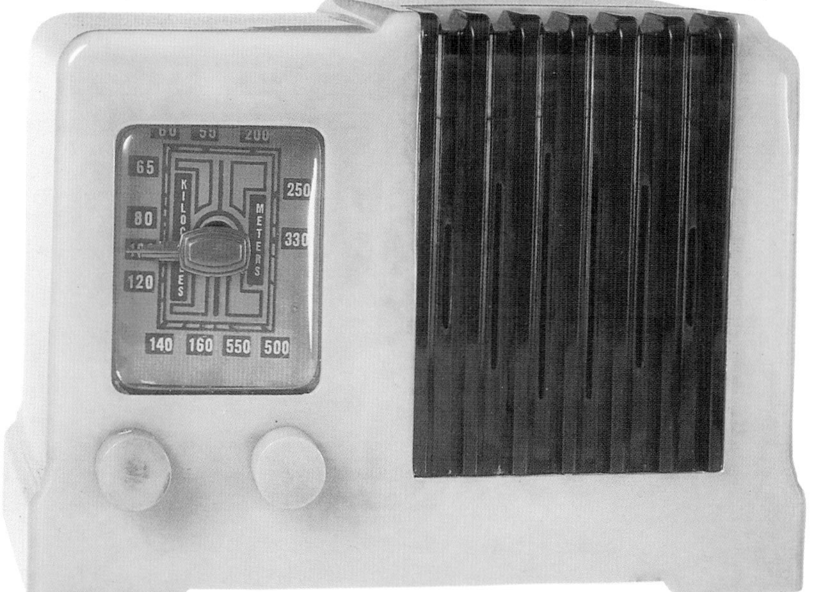

17 Subtly stepped Globe radio. With its vertically ribbed inset grille it is quirky in design and breaks the unwritten rule of putting the speaker to the left. 1938.

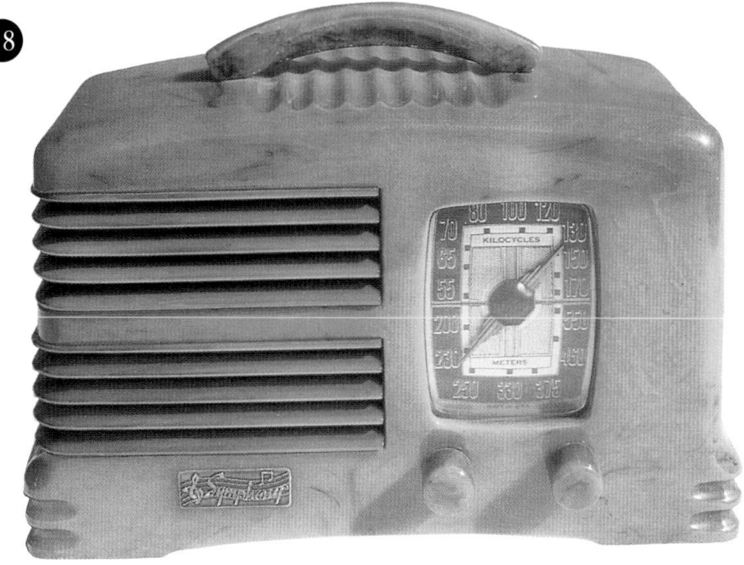

18 Symphony, by Record-O-Vox Inc. One of only two known examples, the color combination of emerald green and butterscotch makes it a radio collector's dream.

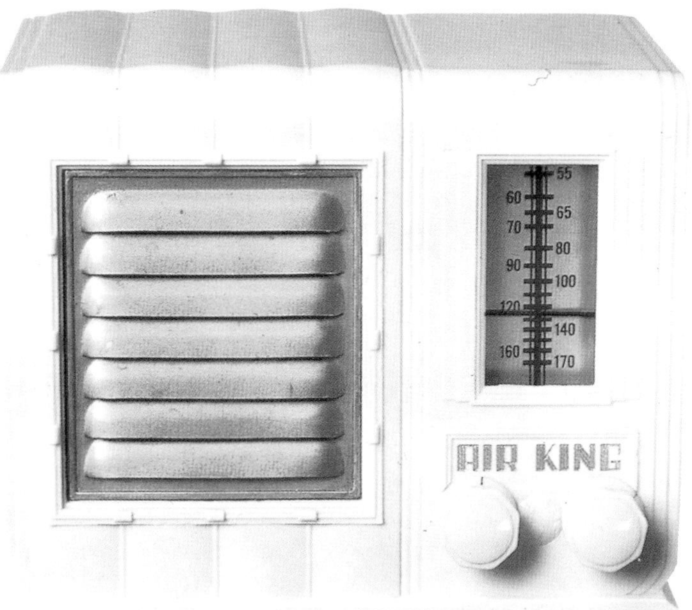

19 *Air King. This baby radio with its anodized metal grille is made of Plaskon, one of the many materials now encompassed by the generic name Bakelite.*

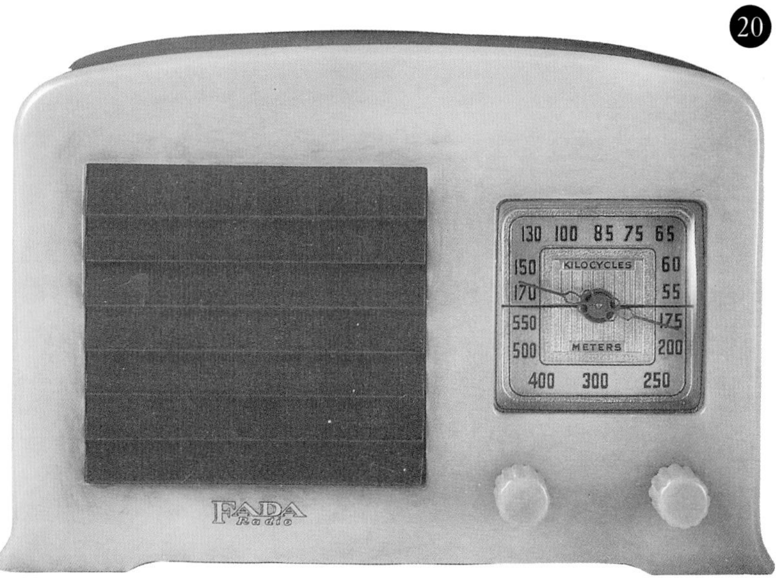

20 *Fada model 53X. Its striking, contrasting cherry-red grille makes this radio much sought after. Usually suffering from tube burn, it is especially difficult to find it in pristine condition due to the proximity of the tubes to the side of the cabinet. 1938.*

21 *Motorola model 52. Its subtle indented geometric line, crisp silver-foiled dial, and contrasting graduating speaker-grille make it striking and desirable. This was Motorola's first venture into Catalin radios. 1939.*

22 *RCA Little Nipper. A solid green lump of Catalin, this small and chunky radio is unusual in that it has no grille-cloth, no celluloid dial-face, and no conspicuous numbers.*

23 *The Temple, by Fada. It came in two very similar models, pre- and postwar. Catalin.*

24

24 *The Bullet, by Fada. This classic streamline was one of the most popular and successful radios ever made. Like the Temple (Fig. 23) it came in both a pre-war gumdrop shape (left) and postwar fluted model (below). Catalin.*

25 *The Bullet, by Fada. This was on occasion produced with a separate contrasting grille. Postwar.*

25

26 De Wald radio. Making up for its moderate size, this monumental and powerful design draws heavily on automobile styling, both interior and exterior. Bakelite. 1940s.

27 A chunky automobile-fender-grilled radio, by Sentinel. Its chassis is usually mounted upside down in its cabinet. 1945.

28 Prewar Garod. Although quite large, it is both attractive and somewhat ingenious with its unique, flush-fitting hideaway drop handle. This particular color combination is the only one known. 1940.

29 *All-American model 188, by Fada. This is surely the scarcest of a number of similar, small, colorful cabinets produced early on by the company, with only a handful known to exist. It was Fada's answer to radios such as Emerson's Patriot, with its red wraparound grille, blue knobs and originally brilliant white cabinet. 1940.*

30 *Motorola Circle Grille model 50XC. It came in a multitude of unusual Catalin colors from this rich honey example to a watermelon red or luxurious emerald green. Like all Motorola's models it is very rare. 1940.*

31 *Five Plus One EP375. Though not the most exciting of Catalin radio designs, this has the unusually inspired feature of six vertical cellulose acetate bars. It was produced in a variety of unconventional colors, sometimes with the inclusion of brass rivets or integral handles. 1941.*

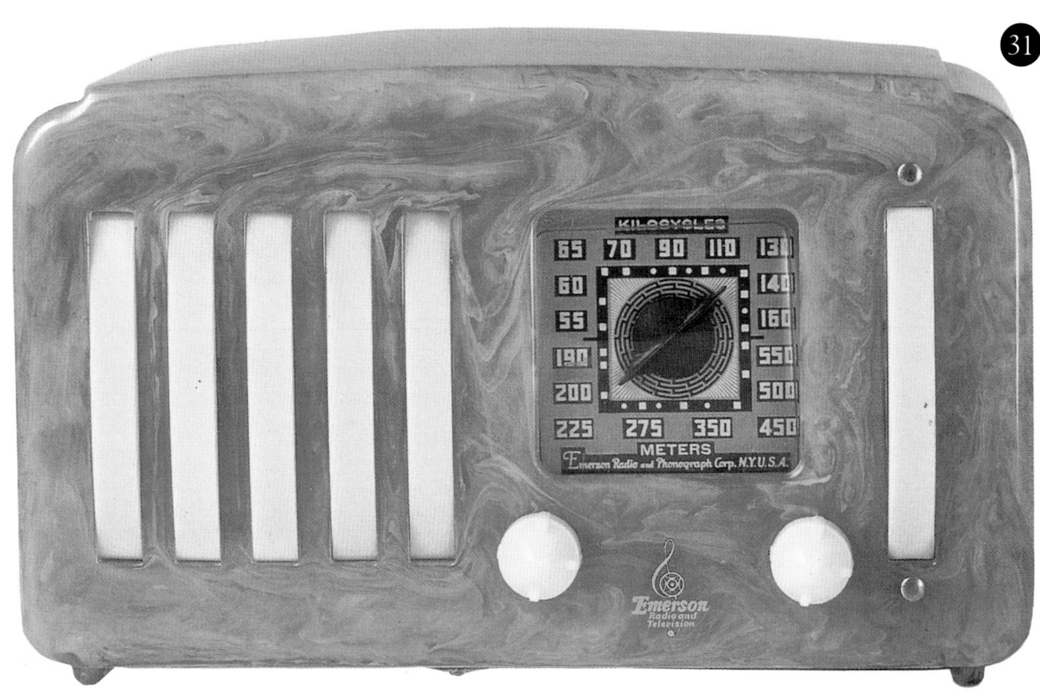

32 *The Patriot, designed by Norman Bel Geddes to celebrate the 25th anniversary of Emerson Radio. It paid obvious homage to the star-spangled banner with its many combinations of red, white, and blue. 1940.*

33

33 Bendix 526C. Although relatively common,it is one of the most robustly constructed radios ever made. Its color combination of green and black as well as its shape are striking and unique in Catalin radio design. 1946.

34

34 Miniature Miracle, by Emerson. The company claimed that it was "The World's Smallest, Power Packed AC-DC Superheterodyne!" This pea-green example was found in mint condition inside its original box. 1947.

35 *Motorola radio, designed by Jean Otis Reinecke. Made in various hues of brown and cream, it has obvious automobile influences and epitomizes the feel of the 1950s.*

35

36

36 *Studebaker-inspired Crosley. It came in a multitude of sometimes striking metallic and non-metallic colors sprayed onto Bakelite. Like a number of other radios of the period, it is evidently influenced by both the grille and the dashboard of the automobile. 1951.*

37 *Zenith Crest. This owl-like radio displays ingenuity of design in its small size and integral frame aerial which is neatly concealed in its liftable handle, and was made in a multitude of different spray-painted Bakelite colors. 1952.*

38 *Model D-25, made by Crosley in Canada. This is both a radio and a wake-up alarm. Made of Bakelite coated with white paint, it is yet another example of the automotive styling that predominated in 1950s radio design. 1953.*

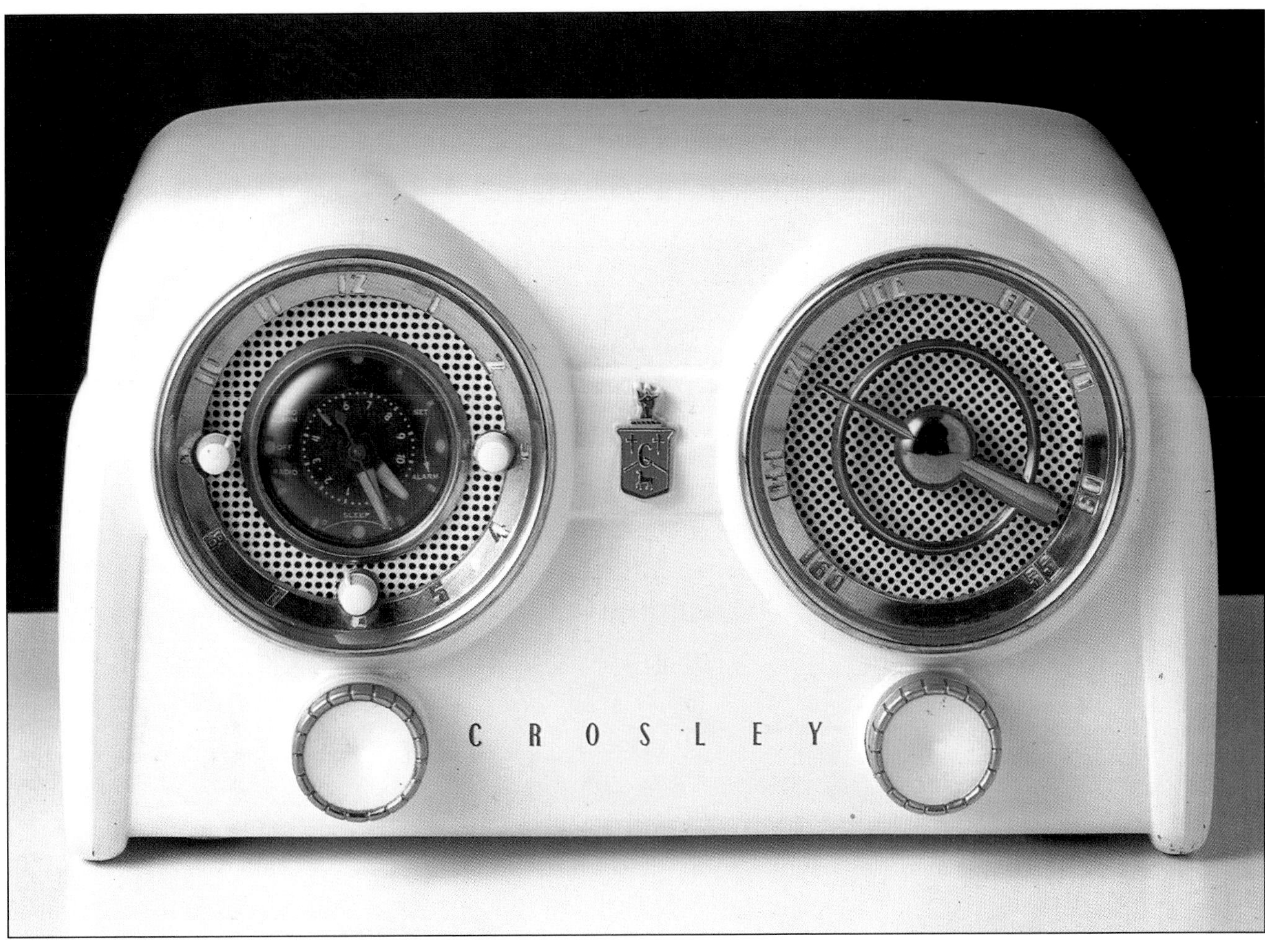

Britain

Radio production in Britain was both extensive and inventive. Beginning in the early thirties, production mainly consisted of large, conservative, brown or black cabinets with the emphasis on design rather than color.

One of the country's most famous radio manufacturers, E.K. Cole of Southend, began life by making traditional wooden radio cabinets. These were assembled in a labor-intensive process by the factory toolworkers or cabinetmakers. The finished product was characteristically a boxlike veneered walnut cabinet which could be subject to warping, cracking, or shrinking, due to the unstable nature of the wood. In 1930, E.K. Cole began to investigate the possibilities of using plastic—specifically Bakelite—as a substitute for wood. Several thousand pounds were committed to buying molding tools and the necessary machinery. It was to prove a worthwhile investment. The firm's turnover increased from £200,000 to £1.25 million in the next six years. Two of the best known in-house designs of E.K. Cole (which was subsequently abbreviated to the trade name "Ekco") are the R2, produced in 1931, and the SH23, manufactured between 1931 and 1933. Both these models would have proved difficult to fabricate in wood. The Bakelite cabinets have rounded corners, with faceted stepping above the speaker grilles. The top of each cabinet is matt-textured. These new designs are quite unlike any previous wooden counterparts. The shapes are not obviously plagiarizing past styles—perhaps the nearest identifiable influence could be described as neo-Egyptian.

In 1934 Ekco took the bold step of engaging design consultants—including the Russian *emigré* Serge Chermeyeff and English architect Wells Coates—to oversee the development of new models. It was Chermeyeff who first produced two innovative new designs, devoid of any traditional references. The use of strong geometrical forms and the striking contrast of a black phenolic-resin casing with chromium-fronted knobs firmly established

1 *Two-tube German-British Burton receiver. Probably the first Art Deco Bakelite radio, it required a separate speaker. 1928–9.*

one of the models as a radio for the modern home. But the use of black phenolic did not prove popular, as it tended to clash with existing warm brown interiors.

A compromise was sought with the introduction of brown and mock walnut finishes. The Wells-Coates-designed, groundbreaking Round Ekco of 1934 represented Britain at its most daring, and Coates continued to design for Ekco. In 1947 he produced the "Princess" radio in green acrylic with a clear, adjustable handle. This design, advanced for its time, foreshadowed developments in the fifties, as radios became less solid and more colorful. Brighter colors involved a change from phenolic resin (phenol-formaldehyde) to urea-formaldehyde, which has a wider color range, including pastels and white. However, early experiments with urea-formaldehyde were not always successful. In 1936 Ekco produced a sample of marbled urea-formaldehyde radio cabinets, but these were subsequently rejected because the urea-formaldehyde looked too cold and stonelike. It was also felt that the cabinets would appear overly heavy and monumental, although this probably has more to do with the large scale and vertical format of the prototypes.

2 *The Masterpiece, by Kolster Brandes. This two-tube model, a "free gift" in return for 5600 Best Dark Virginia cigarette coupons, was one of the first Bakelite radios produced in Britain. 1930.*

3

3 Ekco All-Electric Consolette model R53, by E.K. Cole Ltd. Designed by J.K. White, it was the first British receiver to have a full range of interchangeable station names printed on the dial. Its appearance, with an anodized copper grille, is synonymous with wireless design of the 1930s. 1931.

4 *Model 930A, by Philips. The ham-can-shaped Local Station Receiver was made from Arbolite, an unusual type of plastic-laminated board whose process of manufacture has long been forgotten and which simulated rosewood. It was used on a number of early Philips radios. 1931.*

5 *Radioplayer, by Philips. Heptagonal in shape, this early radio with its oxidized bronze grille is much sought for its outlandish and unique appearance. 1931.*

6 Ekco AC64, by E.K. Cole Ltd. The scale was made adjustable by an interchangeable celluloid dial provided by the manufacturer. New wavelength allocations could be inserted and fixed with studs over the permanent meter scale. 1933.

7 Lissen. This was one of the few radios to have the Egyptian Art Deco look. Well proportioned, it is fragile and therefore rare. 1931.

8 Universal Mains Three, by General Electric Company. One of the few skyscraper radios produced in the United Kingdom, this epitomizes the American culture of its day. 1934.

9 *Philips Superinductance model 830A. It was made from Arbolite, with Bakelite knobs and speaker surround. 1932.*

9

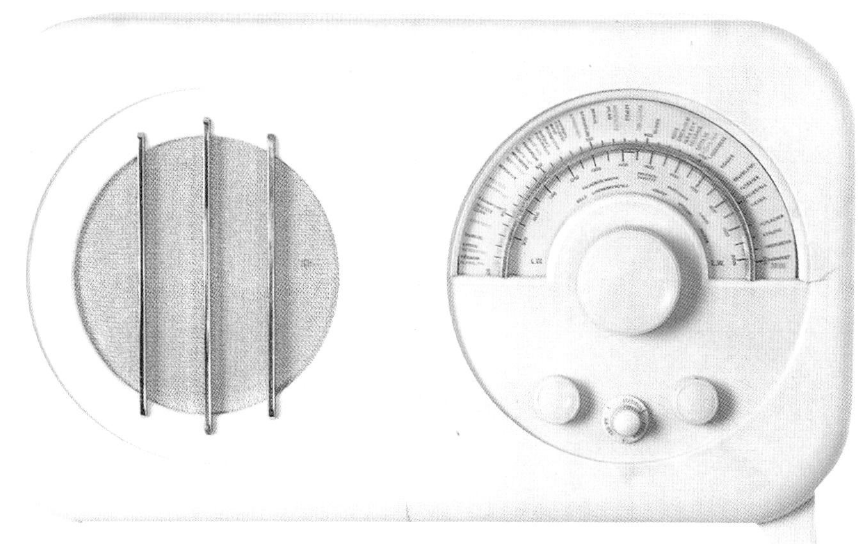

10 *Ekco AC85, by E.K. Cole Ltd. Fragile and possibly unique, this is only one of a handful of "made to special order" colored models. The instability of urea-formaldehyde when molding large expanses has, over the years, caused a number of stress cracks to appear. 1934.*

11 *Ekco AD76, by E.K. Cole Ltd. Now recognized as the most technically accomplished of the Round Ekcos, this is recognizable by its distinct thick horizontal chrome bar, which was sprayed brown for the "walnut" version. 1935.*

12 *Ekco AD36, by E.K. Cole Ltd. This was £3 3s (approximately $4.50) cheaper and 25 percent smaller than its predecessor and is instantly recognizable by its two downwards-curved bars. It was available to special order in a number of non-standard colors such as yellow and blue that are now incredibly rare. 1935.*

13 *The Defiant model M900, produced by the Co-op stores. A radio price-fixing agreement prevented the supply of receivers to the stores because the "dividend" they offered was seen as unfair price-cutting. In response, the Co-op "defiantly" produced their own, uniquely styled radio. 1935.*

14 *Ekco UAW78, by E.K. Cole Ltd. Designed by Misha Black, this is relatively rare, especially in black with chrome trim. 1937.*

15 *Kolster Brandes BM20. A radio designed with economy and thought. It was made of two exact same halves that were then bolted together. Manufactured in a plethora of sometimes quite unique speckled and solid colors, they are now considered a subject for collecting all on their own. 1950.*

16 *Ekco Model AD75, designed by Wells Coates for E.K. Cole Ltd. Fourth of five round radios, it was designed to meet the needs of wartime: "By exercising economy in design, the rising costs of the components have been offset, but no attempt has been made to cheapen either the materials or the finish." Bakelite. 1940.*

17 *Murphy model AD94. Designed by Eden Mins, this radio with its robust, heavily ridged black Bakelite cabinet was manufactured during and after World War II. Its cabinet design remained the same, the only alteration being in 1945 with its change of waveband.*

18 *Ekco A22, by E.K. Cole Ltd. This beautifully thought out finale to the Round Ekco story was produced in "walnut" or black Bakelite with either a "florentine bronze" or chrome loudspeaker surround. Its circular Perspex dial had a traveling cursor that followed around the circumference of the cabinet. It was the culmination of 12 years of production, 14 years of thought and five quite different designs, and resulted in the most logically designed Ekco that brought together both great form and faultless function. 1945.*

19 *The Venus, by Champion. This Perspex sphere with transparent twirly decorations is surely the pinnacle of kitsch. Available in a number of plastic colors, it is often mistaken for Bakelite, though Perspex is a much later plastic. 1947.*

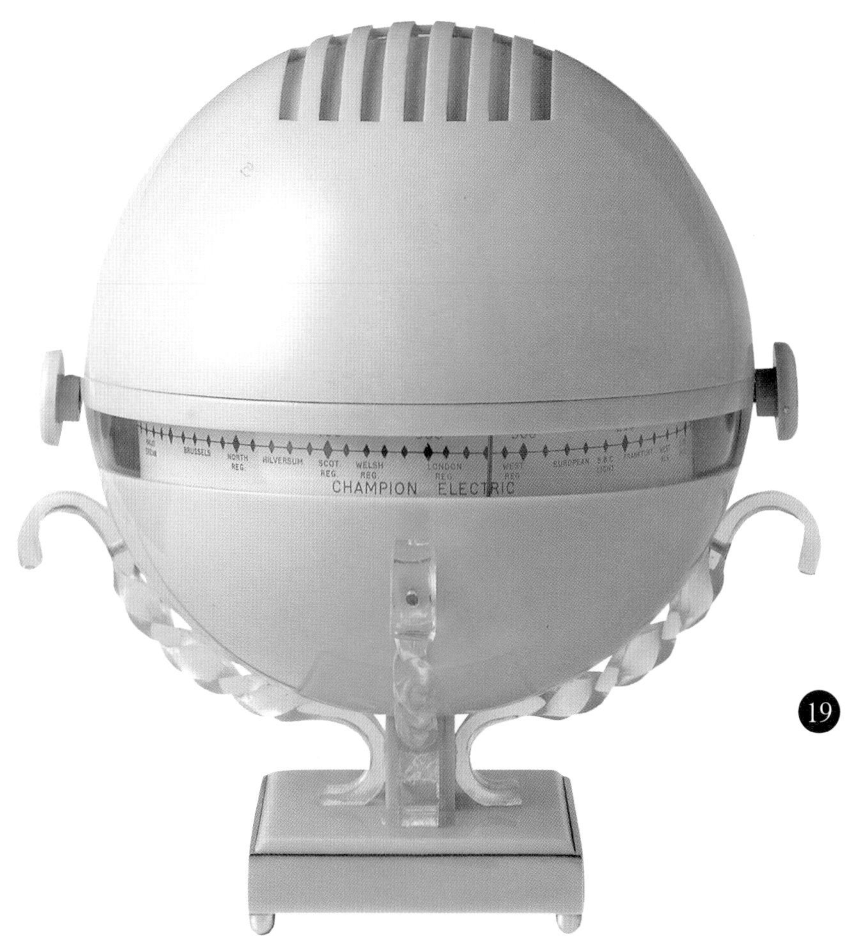

19

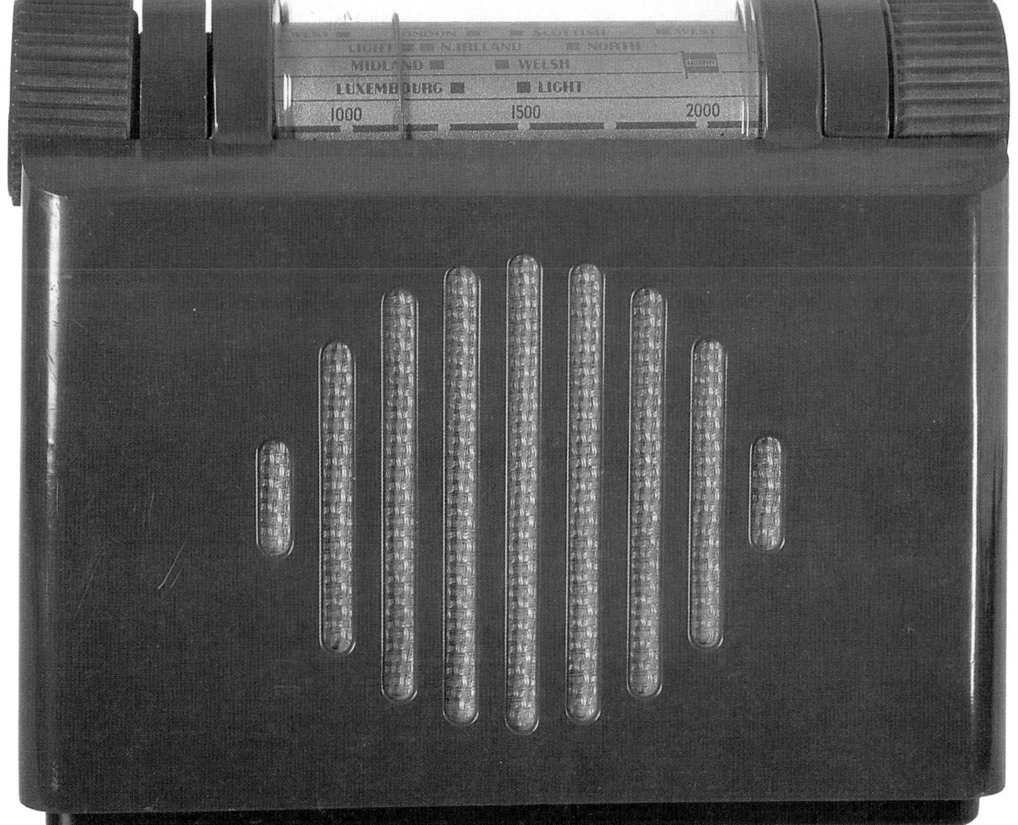

20 *Murphy model A100. Shown at the "Britain Can Make It" exhibition, this burgundy radio is innovative and fresh with its compact, user-friendly, modern design. 1946.*

20

21 *Alba model C112, by A.J. Balcombe Ltd. With its inlaid flower-shaped knobs and contrasting speaker-grille, this comes in a variety of interesting pastel colors, the strongest of which are green and blue. 1947.*

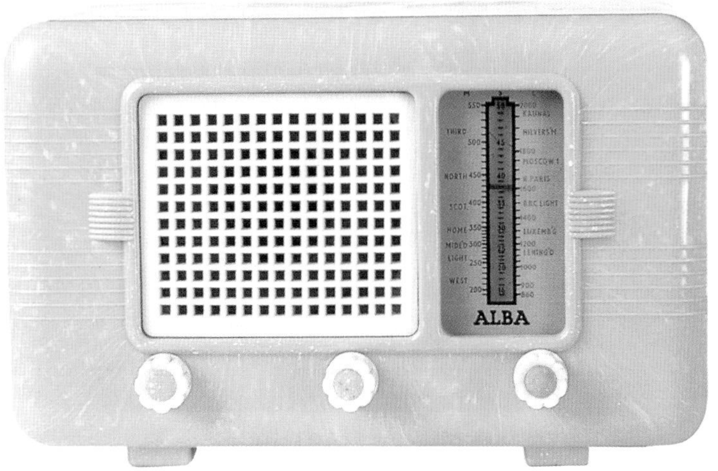

21

22 *Sobellette model 439, by Sobell Industries Ltd. A portable radiator-shaped midget radio that came in a number of sprayed Bakelite finishes. 1949.*

22

23 Kolster Brandes model BM20. A radio designed with economy and thought, it was made of two exact same halves that were bolted together and manufactured in a plethora of sometimes quite unique speckled and solid colors. 1950.

24 *The Toaster, by Kolster Brandes. This midget radio generally had a cream, spray-painted Bakelite case. Other colors like this red one are rare. 1950.*

24

25

25 *Midgetronic. This midget radio came in a number of color combinations, some sprayed on, others solid. In 1953 the cabinet, knobs, and dial were sold separately to enable home-constructors to fit their own chassis. 1950.*

26 *Bush DAC90. More of these seem to have been made than any other Bakelite radio. A variety of models was available from 1946 well into the 1950s in either brown, black, or cream. Although quite common, their straightforward minimalist design makes them both popular and affordable.*

France

With its own definitive style, France produced many uniquely shaped radios, including the series of three postwar mirrored-dial radios produced by the French-American company Sonora. At the leading edge of inventive, innovative design, they were based on the front grilles of flamboyant American automobiles. French radios are highly regarded in many countries.

1 *Radialva radio. France's first Bakelite radio, its bold, geometric cabinet design and delicately decorated grille-cloth hide the simplicity of its construction. Early 1930s.*

2 *Sonora. This large radio looks as though it belongs right in the heart of Paris! Its curved dial, large speaker expanse, and chrome pediments make it stand out as a bold example of Odeon style and design.*

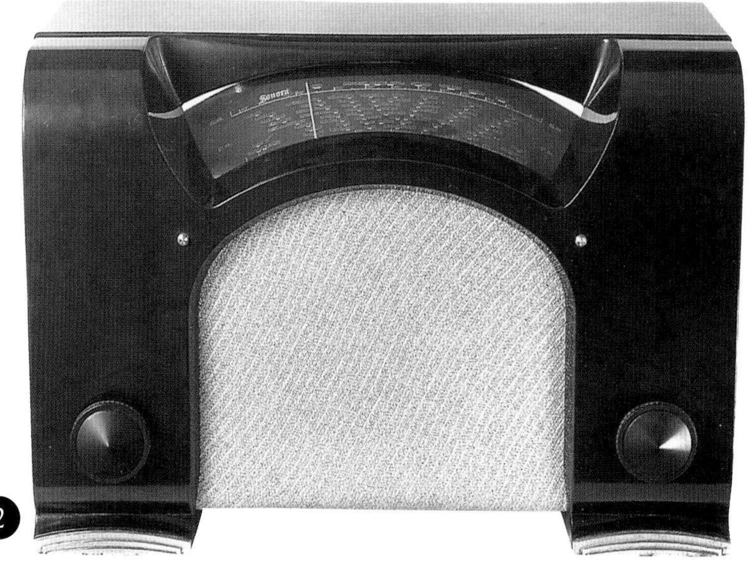

3

3 Sonora radio. With its unique illuminated glass pillars, this robust radio is one of the closest relatives of the larger, more often seen Jukebox. It is quite scarce, especially as the German occupation required all radio receivers to be handed in. 1935.

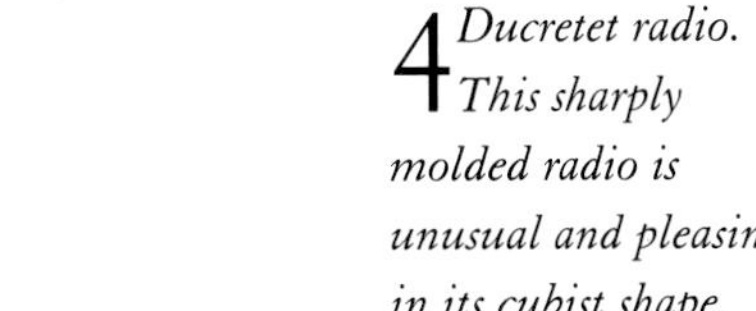

4 Ducretet radio. This sharply molded radio is unusual and pleasing in its cubist shape. It utilizes the company's tuning fork motif, turning it into a striking speaker-grille design. 1934.

5

5 The Super Groom model 41, by Radialva. It displays three wavebands—GO, PO, and OC, or Long, Medium and Short Wave—on its large, oval-shaped glass dial. Late 1930s.

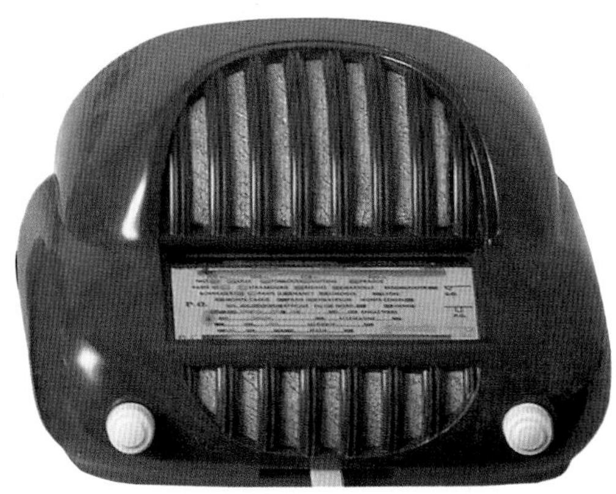

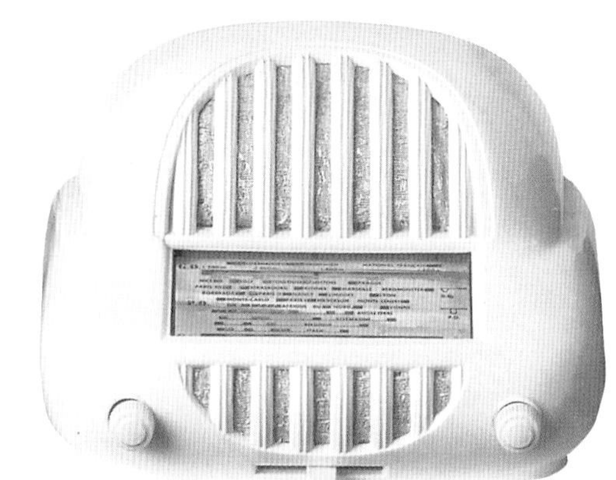

6 Sonorette, by Sonora. Pillow-shaped radios like this, produced by a French-American company, were greatly influenced by the bulbous and curvaceous styling found on American automobiles. It was made in a variety of colors, the green radio being among the scarcest. Late 1940s.

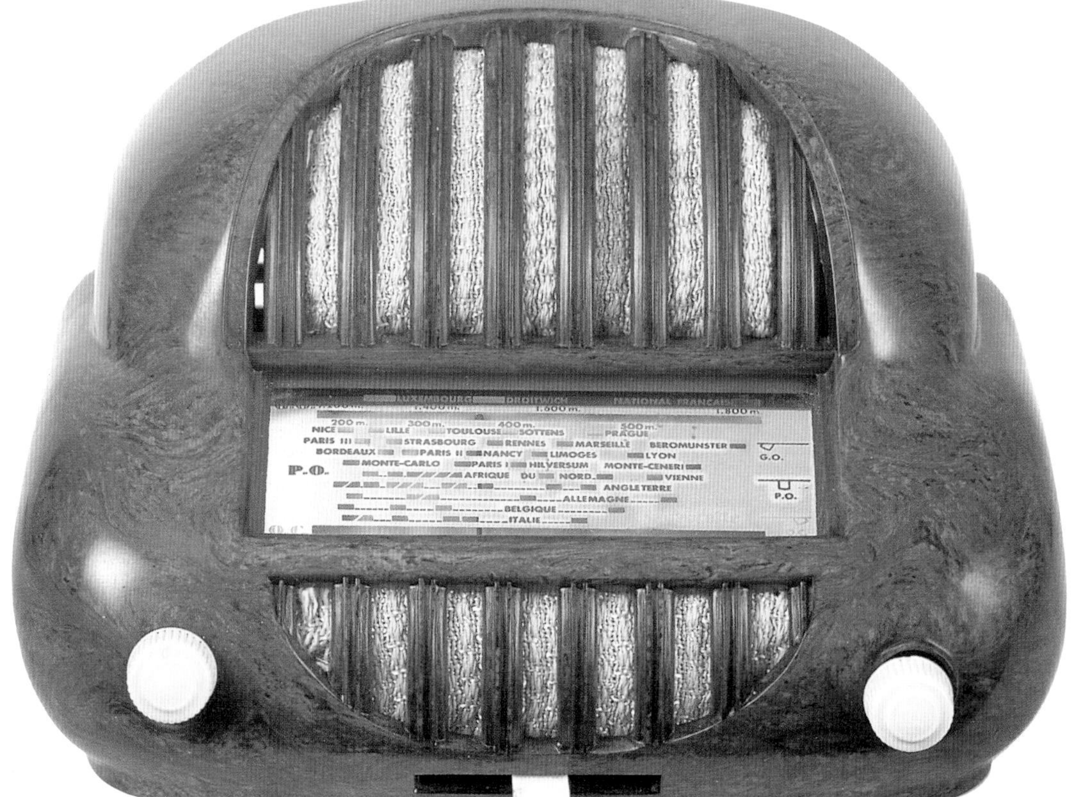

7 Excellence model 301, by Sonora. Known affectionately as "the Cadillac" due to its obvious hoodlike appearance, this radio with its large mirrored dial and chrome trim was American-designed. 1948.

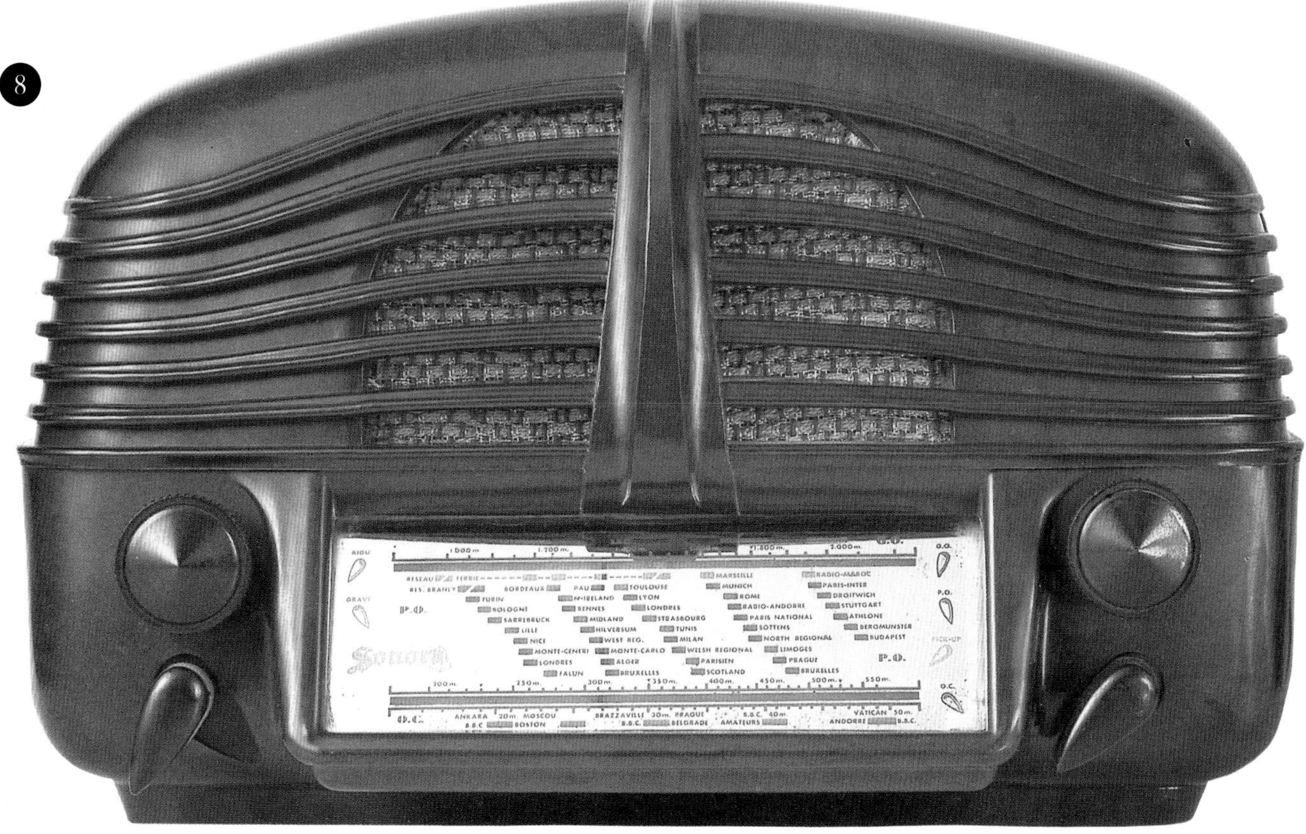

8 Sonora 211. This seems to be a combination of the Sonorette and Cadillac, a rather quirky hybrid.

Germany

The first country to realize the enormous potential of Bakelite in the radio industry, Germany started manufacturing Bakelite sets as early as 1926. Telefunken and Mende produced a large array of bold monolithic radios of a striking form that are relatively scarce today because of the standardization and subsequent confiscation of any set that did not receive the single-waveband propaganda speeches of Hitler's Germany. These mass-produced, economically constructed sets with their Nazi regalia were manufactured in large factories such as Siemens and Telefunken, and are fairly common today.

1 Nora Sonnenblume ("The Sunflower"). This is a spectacular example of the designer's hand running wild. The company was owned by a Jewish family by the name of Aaron, an obvious reversal of "Nora." 1930.

2 Model 148, by Mende. The company manufactured a number of imposing tombstone-shaped radios. This example was produced both in Bakelite and in wood. Early 1930s.

3

3 *Saba radio. The bold design shows an unusual, deeply indented, faceted front and geometrical latticed grille. 1933.*

4

4 *Model 321GL, by Saba. The company produced a substantial array of large radios during the 1930s. They are distinctive for their fretwork-type treatment of the speaker-grille, as in this magnificent example. 1934.*

5 *Lumaphon. The marbleized Beetle trim on this austere radio, reminiscent of the Nazi style of architecture, is very brittle and as a result completely intact examples are hard to find. 1934.*

5

6

6 *The Volksempfanger ("People's Set") VE301GW. The first radio churned out for the masses, it displays an eagle emblem synonymous with the symbols of the Third Reich. 1935.*

7 Deutscher Kleinempfanger ("Small Set"). This was produced by a conglomerate of radio manufacturers. With its centralized eagle-clasping-swastika emblem, it was constructed to receive only stations within the Fatherland, and is now known after Hitler's propaganda minister as the Goebbels Schnauze ("Big Mouth"). On this particular example, an attempt has been made to scratch out the swastika. 1938.

7

8 VE301. The Modernist, upmarket "Party" version of the Kleinempfanger was produced in the year of the Anschluss. As Austria and Germany joined so did the station names on the radio's dial. The swastika on this set is clearly visible. 1938.

9 DAF tuner-amplifier. This was used in German factories, connected to public address systems to provide music to aid productivity. It also relayed Nazi propaganda—particularly Hitler's speeches, which were compulsory listening during the war. 1938.

Italy

A limited number of receivers were manufactured in Italy during the pre- and postwar years due to the country's deep financial recession. This resulted in a none-too-prolific radio industry making the majority of their radios in wood. When Bakelite was used, the inventiveness and strength of design was outstanding, as with Castiglioni's sculptural Phonola of 1939 (see page 70).

1 *Phonola 557. Although not prolifically manufactured, Italian radios exude their own style of design. The four wavebands on this robust example light up individually when a specific column is selected for tuning. 1937.*

2 *Radiomarelli. Known affectionately as "the Fido," this takes its styling directly from compact American prewar radios such as the Emerson and RCA midgets. 1939.*

The influence of technology

The design of Bakelite objects was influenced to a large extent by the technical requirements of the molding process. The object could not be designed so that it was locked into the mold and therefore difficult to remove. A common general rule was that objects should taper towards the deepest part of the mold, or alternatively the object was molded in separate pieces (an extractor fan, for example, might have as many as seven individually molded components). The inner surface of the mold could be employed to create a variety of finished textures—matt or shiny, even rough grain in an imitation of natural materials such as leather. After the molding process was completed, any rough edges, flash lines or uneven surfaces were sanded down, filed or polished. Decorative motifs or brand names could be added by means of inserts. Knockout pins employed to loosen the object from the mold could leave marks, but were generally positioned so as to be unobtrusive.

Molds had to be carefully designed so that the molten Bakelite would flow evenly and completely into the mold. Sharp corners proved impractical and were thus avoided, giving rise to the smooth, "streamlined" style popular in the thirties. The walls of the mold had to be of equal thickness to allow a free flow of material and to avoid the risk of distortion when the Bakelite shrank as it hardened and cooled. If this proved unavoidable, ribs were incorporated to provide additional strength. Thick walls also took more time to cool and harden, a factor which had to be considered by the designer in order to make the most efficient use of machines.

Excellence model 301, by Sonora. Bakelite. Late 1940s.

Spain

1 *Model 1065, by Telefunken. The German company set up a factory in Madrid where it produced a multitude of radios both pre- and postwar. This radio seems to take its inspiration from the wooden harp. Its brown Bakelite case is ridged and indented with gold-painted lines.*

Civil war and poverty laid to rest any plans of Bakelite radio production in Spain, which only got going in the postwar forties when a number of large foreign manufacturers set up factories in both Madrid and Barcelona producing Spanish variants of current models. When homegrown designers were finally allowed a free hand in the mid-fifties, a number of striking shapes appeared.

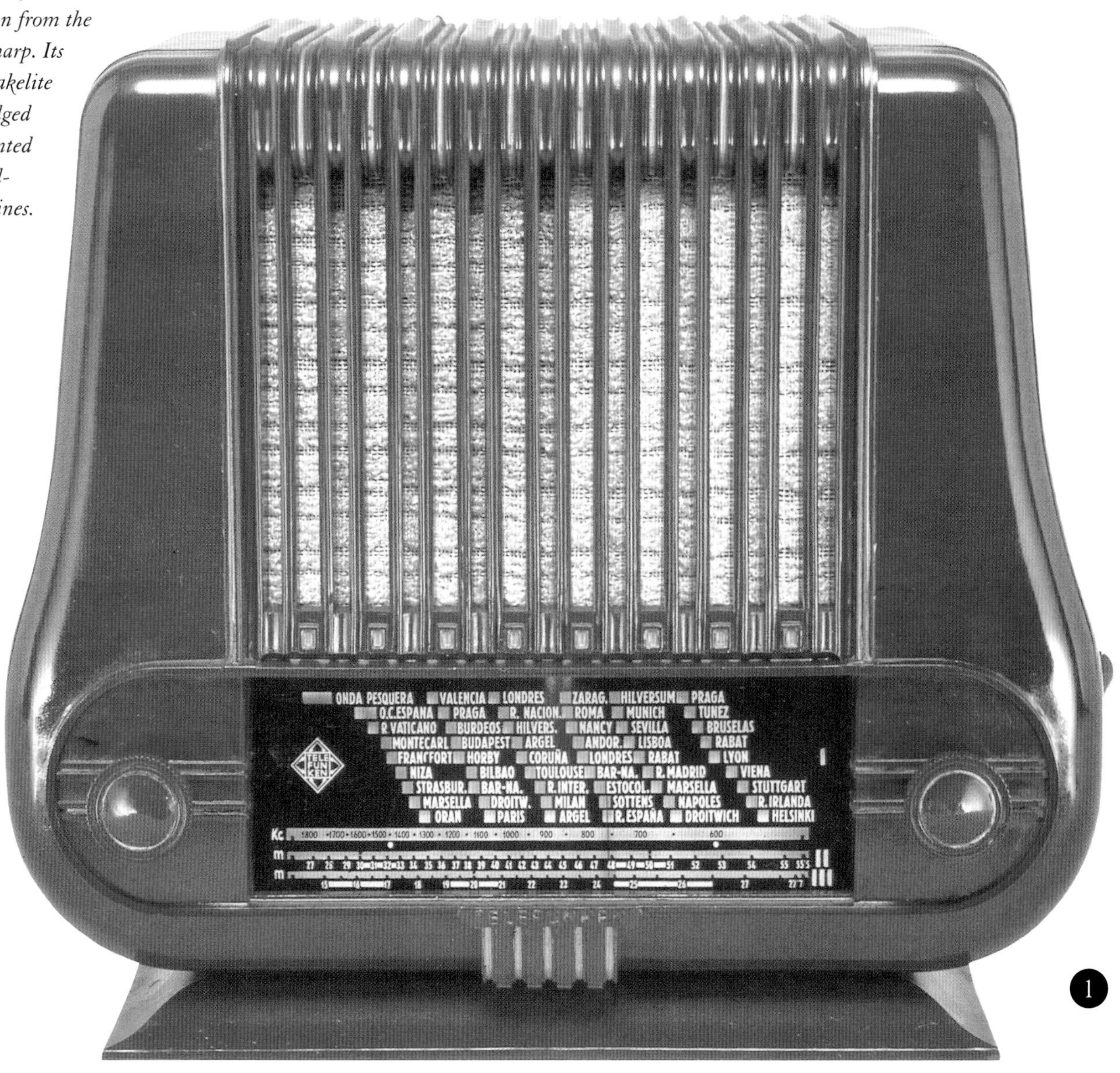

1

2 *Suminístrado. This factory-painted deep red radio was marketed in kit form for home enthusiasts to assemble. Mid-1940s.*

3 *Model BE 312U, by Philips. Among other companies, Philips set up a factory in Barcelona where they produced this highly stylized miniature, sunburst design. 1952.*

4 *Model U1515, by Telefunken. A striking, bulbous white radio. Mid-1950s.*

Czechoslovakia

A number of major factories were based in Czechoslovakia in the years preceding World War II. As well as their own Europe-wide models a number of variants were manufactured, such as the charming Philips Butterfly of the mid-thirties. Following the Occupation, Bakelite radio production all but ceased. As a result many examples have been well used and are therefore in poor condition.

1 Model 964AS, by Philips. This rather small radio, known as "the Butterfly" for obvious reasons, was manufactured locally and is considered rare today. Early 1930s.

2 Tesla Talisman. Highly desirable in Iron Curtain days, this streamlined radio has now turned up in great numbers. Although it was designed in the 1930s it was only put into production in the late 1940s.

Australia

Not well known for its radio industry, Australia produced a number of stunning architecturally inspired radios such as the monumental AWA Radiolette, which when found in its soapy green variety epitomizes the color and feel of its age. The very small population of Australia resulted in a limited production run of each model.

1 *General Electric radio. Usually found bearing the AWA Radiolette insignia, this was the first Bakelite radio manufactured in Australia. With its ornate Art Nouveau cabinet and spiraling knobs, it must surely be one of the most exciting brown Bakelite radios ever manufactured. 1932.*

2 Radiolette. Modeled on the Australian Wireless Association's office building in Sydney, this radio with its deeply indented, bulbous ridges is typical of the Empire State skyscraper style. 1930s.

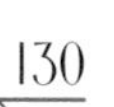

3 Astor. The organic-looking dial is a unique feature of this radio's design. The color changes from blue to yellow when the frequency band is switched. Mid-1930s.

4 *Fisk Radiolette. The contrasting green fretwork grille and feet set against its lustrous black Bakelite body make the design of this dual-waveband radio stand out.*

4

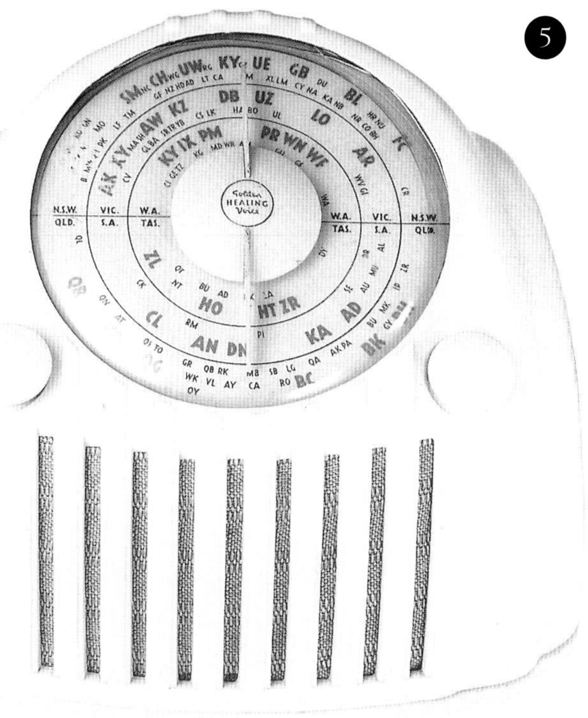

5

5 *The Healing Moderne. Manufactured in either brown, white, or occasionally green, this is often referred to as the "bathroom scales model." With its enormous dial and automobile-fender-grille front, it is surely one of the most over-powering designs ever produced. 1950.*

6 *The Astor Football. This was produced in a multitude of pastel shades as well as the more-often-found brown. As with a majority of Australian radios, different dials were supplied, depending on which state you lived in. This one is for New South Wales.*

6

Modernism

The potential of plastics as a source of relatively inexpensive consumer goods was not fully realized until the thirties and the advent of Modernism—a doctrine that remained influential until well after World War II. This movement in architecture and design, inspired by the Functionalist tenets of the influential German Bauhaus school of design and the Swiss architect Le Corbusier, acknowledged and embraced the dramatic changes taking place in technology and industry. As the desire for change gained impetus, the demand for large quantities of goods gave birth to the technology of mass production and unlike many traditional materials, plastic proved ideally suited to the new processes.

The Modern Movement in architecture and design had been gradually gaining ground in Europe since the first decade of the twentieth century. In 1909, the Italian Futurists, a group of avant-garde artists, published a manifesto calling for a rejection of past stylistic values which were considered intellectually and aesthetically bankrupt. In a treatise that was to prove hugely influential in European art and architecture, the Futurists endorsed the notion of "dinamismo," literally the "dynamic of the machine." In 1914 the Italian Futurist architect Antonio San'Elia visualized a house "like a giant machine ... enriched only by the innate beauty of its lines ... extraordinarily beautiful in its mechanical simplicity ..." This potent vision was crystallized by Le Corbusier into the influential tenet, "A house is a machine for living in."

Underpinning these radical pronouncements was a heightened sense of social responsibility and a firm commitment to the democratizing effects of mass production, standardization, and the application of new industrial materials, such as plastic, steel, and concrete.

The extremely popular Bush DAC90 was mass-produced during the late 1940s and early 1950s in cream urea-formaldehyde as well as black and brown solid and mottled Bakelites. Variations also occurred in the different grille-cloths, metal gauze speaker-covers and different-colored grilles. 1948.

Jewelry

Originally a substitute for more expensive materials such as ivory and coral, plastic jewelry flourished widely during the Jazz Age of the twenties and thirties. The new spirit of the times cheerfully dispensed with straitlaced Victorian ideas about personal adornment which had previously stressed the minimal use of jewelry. Encouraged by such flamboyant pioneers as Coco Chanel, Elsa Schiaparelli and Nancy Cunard, it became fashionable for women to wear large quantities of bracelets, pins, necklaces, and assorted trinkets. Plastics were lightweight, durable, easy to manufacture, and ideally suited for mass production. The inherent decorative potential of materials such as Bakelite and Catalin began to be exploited by designers, with frequently startling results.

Phenolic resins used in jewelry were generally cast as rods, tubes, and slabs which were then sliced into individual pieces. These "blanks" were shaped and carved on lathes and drills in a method similar to glass etching. Because of the excellent heat resistance of phenolics, the pieces could withstand the friction of the grinding machinery without melting or becoming distorted. Designs followed many themes—exotic floral and geometric patterns in the Art Deco style were popular. It has been said that it was a style made for plastics, which were often dramatically combined with other materials such as rhinestones, metal, wood, or glass In the early thirties, Bakelite jewelry could be found in most prestigious department stores around the world, including Saks in New York, Harrods in London, and the Galeries Lafayette in Paris. In 1935, Macey's, the New York store, made it the subject of a special window display. A year later it was estimated that two-thirds of all costume jewelry was made from Bakelite. New York artists Belle Kogan and Martha Sleeper used Bakelite jewelry to celebrate American culture, exploiting a range of diverse motifs from baseball and Uncle Sam to President Roosevelt's Scottie dog. Josephine Baker, the outrageous darling of the Paris Folies Bergères, made presents of specially commissioned Bakelite jewelry featuring miniature compacts, lipsticks, and even peacock feathers. French design house Cartier produced watches with Bakelite cases and topical events inspired the Alta Novelty Company of Manhattan to make Bakelite Union Jack pins for the coronation of King Edward VIII in 1936. More than fifty years on, the color and style of Bakelite jewelry has come back into fashion, with avid collectors scouring auction houses and junk shops in the hope of finding that elusive rare specimen.

Accessories included umbrella handles, handbag frames, and belts. Clips and belt buckles are among some of the nicest carved pieces and tend to blend in with other pieces of jewelry. Indeed, designers coordinated sets to tempt the consumer—earrings, necklace, pin, dress clips, ring, and buckle.

Bracelets

Plain, uncarved bangles led the way onto the fashion scene in the mid-twenties, and from these jewelry-makers developed basic pieces that had been turned and carved on a lathe to give them a bit of dimension. Bangles soon progressed into the single-dimension flower and leaf stage and, as the skills of the carvers grew keener, they were given coats of finely, or dramatically, carved scenes: a panorama, a seascape of a beach scene with a few palm trees, the setting sun, and a bird or two searching the waves for dinner. There are bracelets that are totally carved in the texture of pineapples; and there are pieces with heavily carved tropical vegetation—large flowers with leaves and stems—all in very deep relief. Other designs correspond to the Art Deco or Machine Age and were actually done in patterns resembling gears and sprockets. These geometrics took their place in Bakelite jewelry as they had in other areas of the decorative arts.

A sibling to the geometric approach is the stripe bracelet. This was generally uncarved but there was the "can't leave it alone" breed of designer who just had to facet it, or put it on a lathe to score it a bit. Polka-dot bracelets were generally done in extremely contrasting color schemes. Black with white (now mustard as a result of oxidization), black with pink (now orange), mostly with dark tubes and light dots, or vice versa. Unfortunately, the polka dot has caught the brunt of the "new" or made up Bakelite scare.

The hinged bracelet is the byproduct of cutting a tube in half, and ultimately joining the two pieces, with a spring-loaded hinge which was fastened to the Bakelite with screw or pins. The opposite side of the hinged portion opens, and this type of bracelet can easily be slid across the wrist, thereby alleviating the need for a large opening. The elastic or stretch bracelet is exactly what it sounds like, a conglomeration of Bakelite pieces that were drilled and held together by an elasticized string which was drawn through the holes and knotted.

Finally, there are the "fantasy bracelets." They encompass all the crazy, wacky, fun pieces that cannot be listed under the previously mentioned headings and include mostly fruits and vegetables and other dangly items. Most of these had Bakelite pieces that were hung from metal or celluloid chains. There were also charm bracelets made with Bakelite pieces. Unfortunately, these are very rare today, mostly because they were of a more delicate nature than other pieces and could not stand the test of time.

The carver's skills

A square bangle with an oval hole. Plain-colored bracelets were produced in a vast variety of shapes.

Early Bakelite bangles were simple, but soon the better carvers were given more complex designs to reproduce. After the bangle was appropriated from the tube, it was put onto a jigging machine, which consisted of an indexing head, in order to calibrate the carving into windows or scenic sections. The actual carving was done with a range of tools. Sometimes the piece was put on a lathe and turned to the desired pattern. Often a rotary-type tool with various styled bits was used in conjunction with a tracery mechanism or guide to cut the less complicated patterns (for instance, a leaf and flower). The more complicated heavy-relief pieces were pattern-scribed first, then were extended freehandedly with a rotary-type tool. This could be used to carve and get under the back of, say, a rose, so that the petals have the relief, or 3-D effect, found on some of the "big" or "heavy" carved items. This rotary tool was also utilized freehand, to carve most of the "reverse-carved" pieces.

Simple-striped bangles.

After the carving was finished for the day, most of the work was tumbled in huge drums filled with fillers and various grit silica. Each batch went through a rough, medium, and fine process, before a final detergent and polishing stage. Some of the "heavy" carved pieces were polished with a cloth or felt wheel using a pumice solution, to diminish any "wheel," or carving marks before engaging in the cleaning and polishing stages. A few select pieces had the extreme edges finely polished, after dancing with a medium grit solution in the tumbler. This would leave the edges with a glasslike finish, with the inner depths of the carving in a matt-like or frosted finish. This is an extremely beautiful effect, especially on some of the clear pieces.

2 *Hinged and striped bangles.*

1 *Two-tone bangles. A multitude of designs and techniques was used to produce striped pieces like these.*

3 *Thin two-tone bangles.*

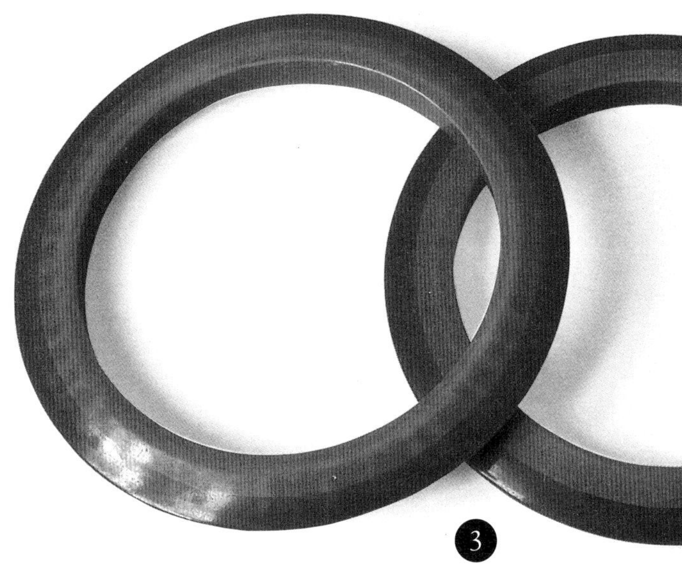

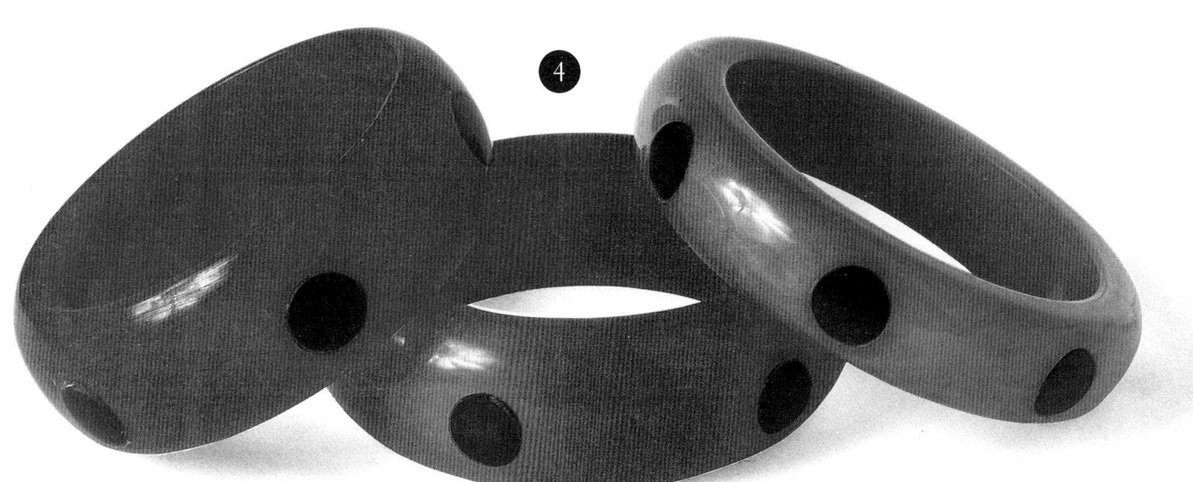

4 *Polka-dot bangles. Possibly one of the most fun and whimsical designs of the era, circles of one color are shown against a contrasting background.*

6 Clear and opaque bangles with polka-dot inserts.

7 Pairs of plain bangles. Extremely popular, these were generally worn as spacers or as a group of as many as eight.

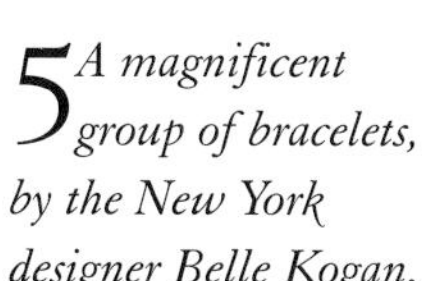

5 A magnificent group of bracelets, by the New York designer Belle Kogan. She took the polka dot, stretched it into an oval, and progressively elongated this figure.

8 "Stretchy" or elastic bracelets. These generally tend to be fairly simple designs, using plain pieces of Catalin.

9 Striped bangles. These were cast half and half.

10 Elastic bracelets. Two or three different shapes and sizes of plastic are used.

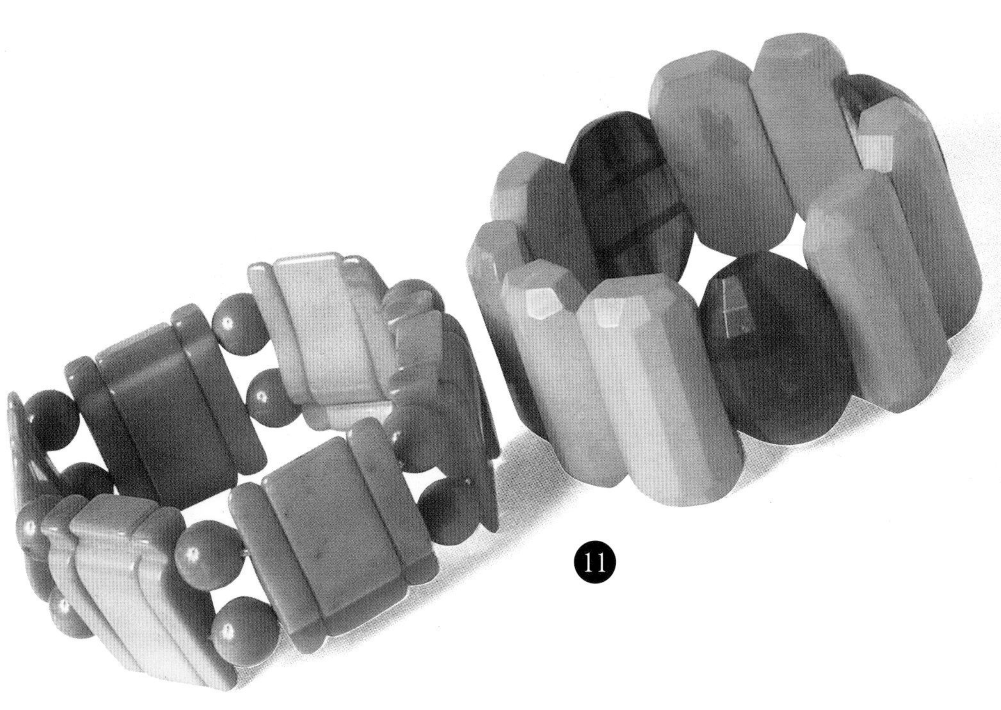

11 *"Stretchy" bracelets. Simple, but fun designs.*

12 *Spectacular group of hinged geometric and laminated bracelets. These are possibly of European origin.*

13 Domino bracelets. These are considered to be "new" Catalin but anyone knowledgeable can see that they are old gaming pieces.

14 Mah-jong bracelets. Like the domino pieces, they are considered to be "new" Catalin.

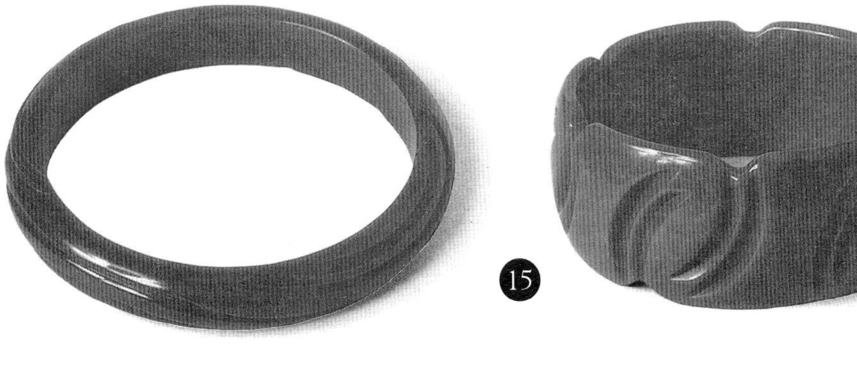

15 Simply-scored bangles. The amount of carving and intricacy varied from piece to piece.

16 Magnificent green bangle that was turned on a lathe. Its plastic-coated string is still intact.

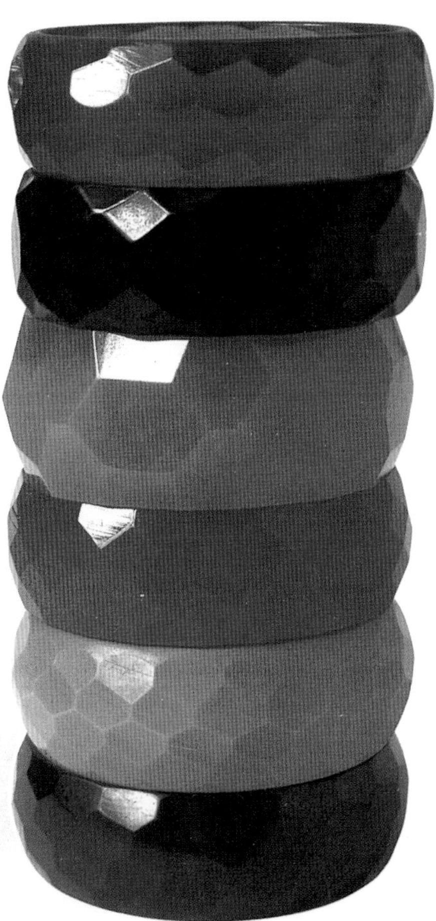

17 Carved bangles. The regular stripes were scored on a lathe.

18 A stack of faceted bangles. The technique was popular on both clear and opaque pieces.

19 Bangles turned on a lathe. Some were produced in just one color while others were dyed after carving.

20 *Bracelets with heavy-carved reliefs. Leaves and flowers were popular motifs.*

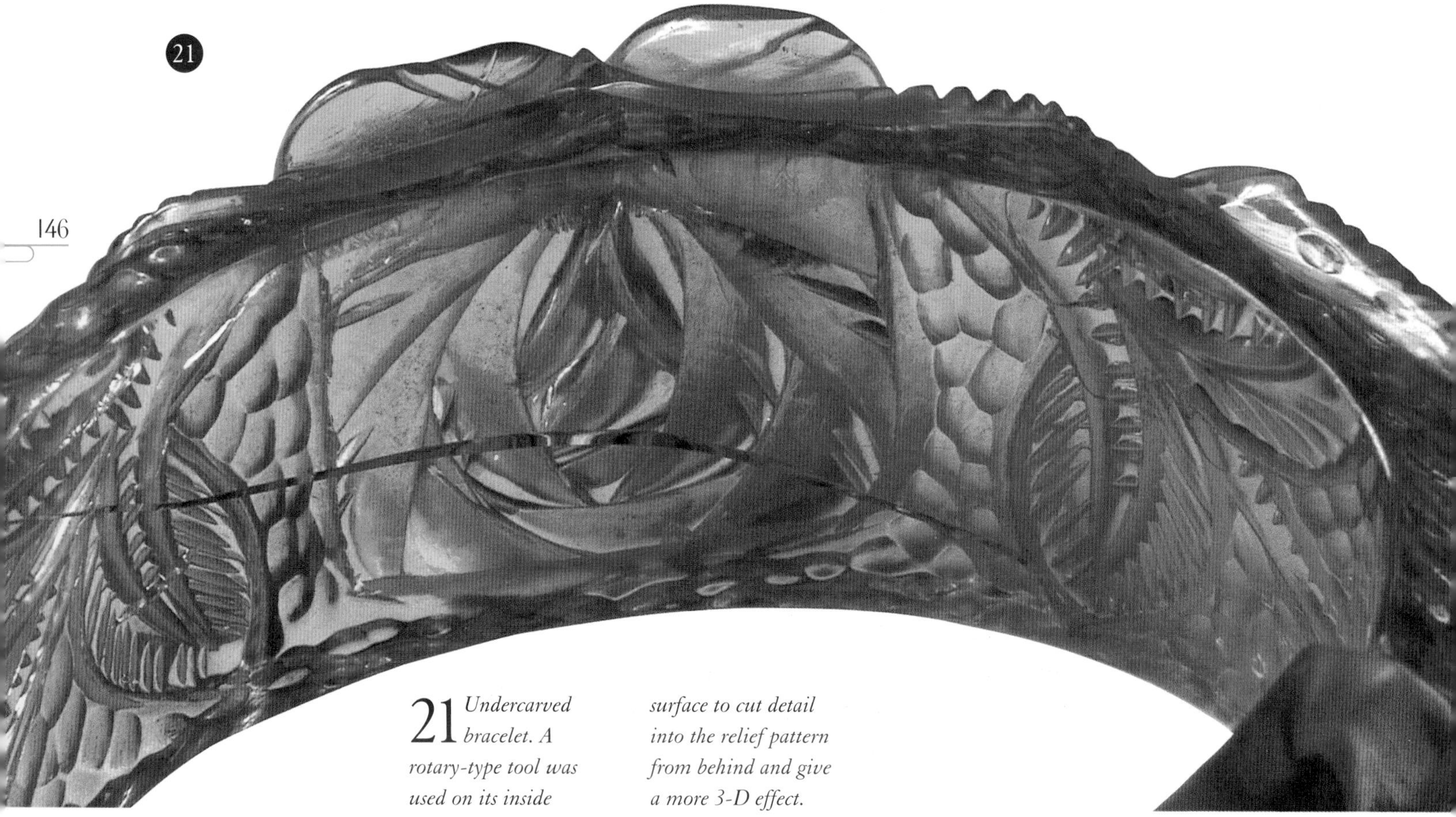

21 *Undercarved bracelet. A rotary-type tool was used on its inside surface to cut detail into the relief pattern from behind and give a more 3-D effect.*

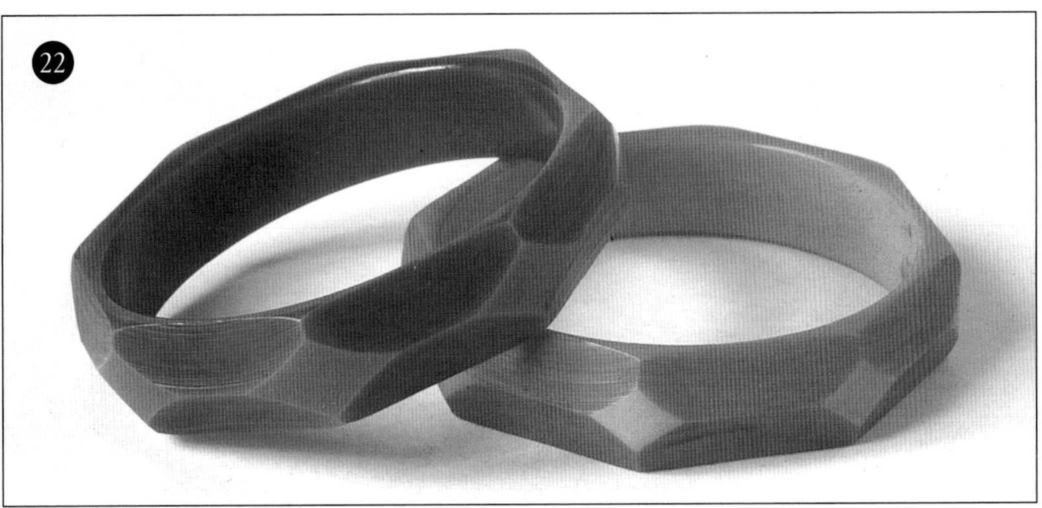

22 *A pair of geometrically designed white bangles. They show varied oxidation.*

23 *Faceted bangles. It became fashionable to wear up to seven or eight pieces on one arm.*

24 *Carved bangle. A tracery mechanism was used to cut the pattern.*

25 *Simply-carved bangle. The window effect was created using an index head.*

26 *Undercarved bangle. The technique was applied to clear Bakelite and the relief was then painted.*

27 *Stack of clear unpigmented bangles. While a couple are plain, there are some that show the progression to carving simple flower designs.*

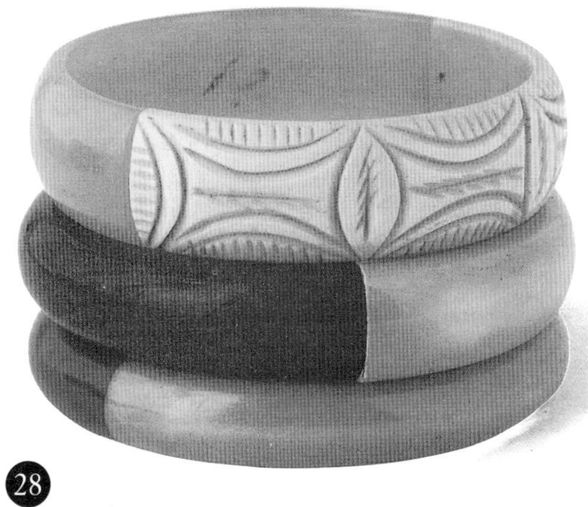

28 *Carved and striped bangles.*

29 *Stack of heavy-carved bangles. Flowers and leaves seem to be predominant designs.*

30 *Impressive tower of white and butterscotch heavy-carved bangles. The white ones have darkened through oxidation.*

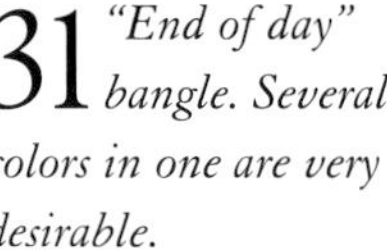

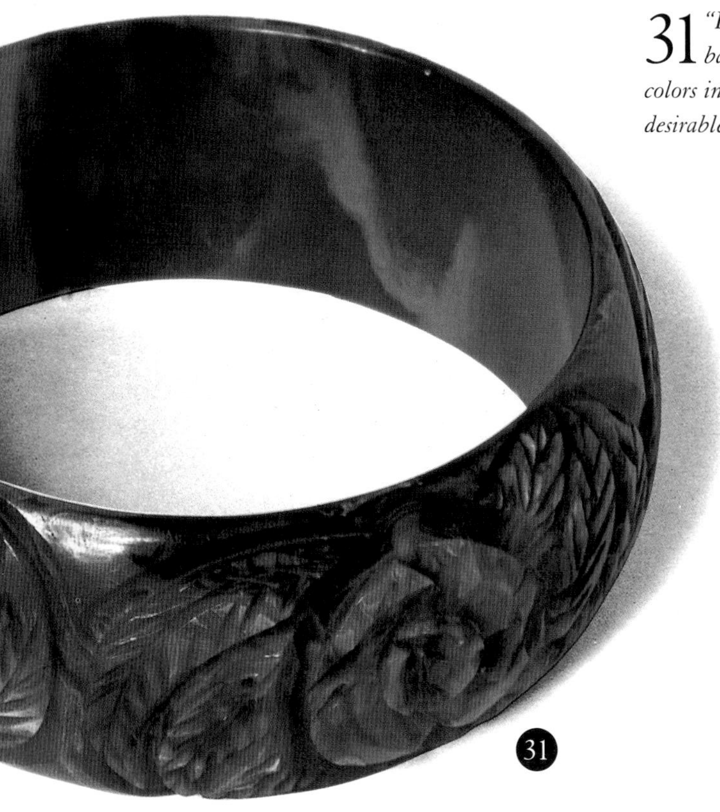

31 "End of day" bangle. Several colors in one are very desirable.

32 Stack of heavy-carved bangles. These show the extreme intricacy of some designs.

33 A group of heavy-carved hinged bracelets.

34 *A selection of bangles, showing the same design in different colors; the same design in the same colors; and the same design in different colors and widths.*

36 *White carved hinged bracelet and pin. Both are inset with a black Bakelite cameo.*

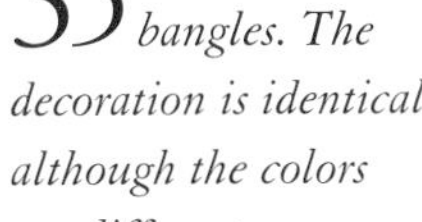

35 *Tower of carved bangles. The decoration is identical although the colors are different.*

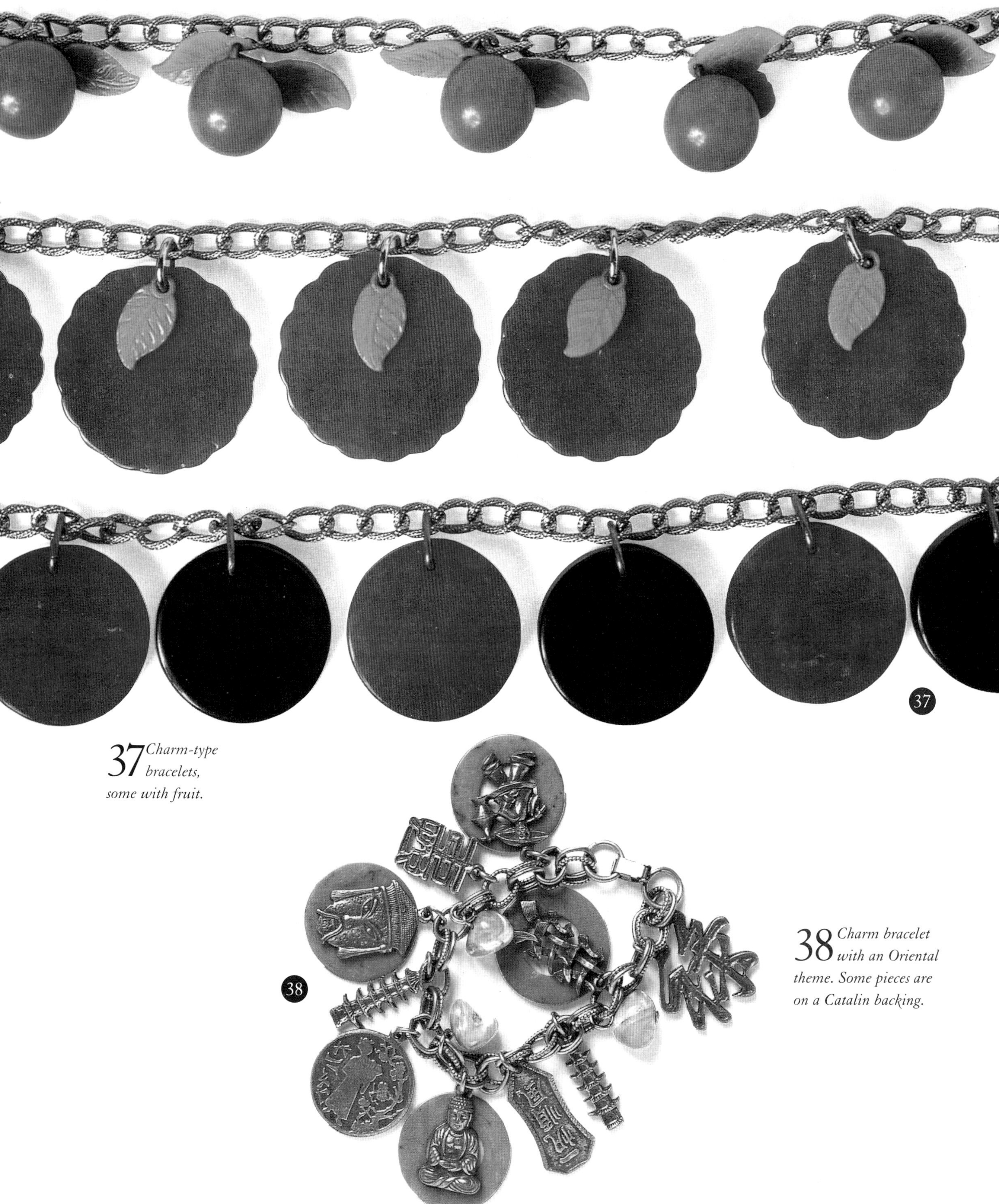

37 Charm-type bracelets, some with fruit.

38 Charm bracelet with an Oriental theme. Some pieces are on a Catalin backing.

Pins, brooches, and accessories

Pins are the devil-may-care members of the Bakelite jewelry family. The original ones were totally plain white (now mustard), black, or brown. It can be seen that some of these were wrought from the sides of tube stock. As engineers and chemists advanced the color range the pin was soon given a wardrobe of glamorous color. Layers of these colors were added as soon as the laminating process was perfected and the pin rapidly expanded into lavish carvings as well as some of the Machine Age shapes found in its older sibling, the bracelet.

In America and Europe a flurry of animals was produced. They formed a huge proportion of the Bakelite pins. Some were in their natural state while others took on personalities. It was possible to wear a favorite wildlife animal or a whimsical family pet, an insect or a bird, a horse's head, or a carousel pony. Every animal imaginable has been immortalized in Bakelite, from anteater to zebra, both as a normal characterization and dressed up in clothing with a set of great goggly eyes. But the one that sits on the top of the sales charts must be the Scottie. Fashioned after President Roosevelt's pet, Fala, the Scottie pins are worked in all the ifferent colors, from simple to detailed, serious to totally whimsical. Scotties were manufactured all over the globe.

When the Machine Age vein branched out from the Deco era it took the European market in that direction, while American craftsmen were left to the "fun and games" portion of the industry. From Europe came the serious angular style that was associated with this avenue of Art Deco. The French were pushing out tremendous pieces, vibrant colors with trimmings of chrome, or accented with equally colorful, but contrasting, crystal stones.

The Germans, meanwhile, trimmed some of the pieces in brass. They also took a liking to laminating transluscent and opaque colors with clear ones. Some of the most stylistically great pieces attributed to them are the tool pieces, which have a number of tools with Catalin handles dangling from a Catalin bar pin. The tools actually work.

The bar pin was the first of the brooches to be created. Initially somewhat plain, it was later carved and eventually took on the shape of a ribbon and even a bow. As designers started to get bored with the everyday carving of the pins, they ventured, into creating fantasy pieces. Accessories like dress clips and belt buckles simulate some of the designs of bangles or pins. You as a collector can spend months in search of these decorative pieces to complete a set.

Pins and brooches

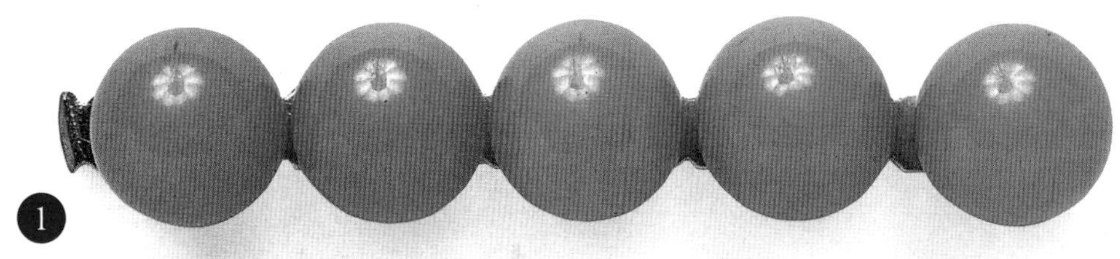

1 *A simple geometric sphere pin.*

2 *A heavy geometric pin.*

3 *Very simple "hoops" in a range of different colors.*

4 *Very simple butterscotch bar pin with a little scoring.*

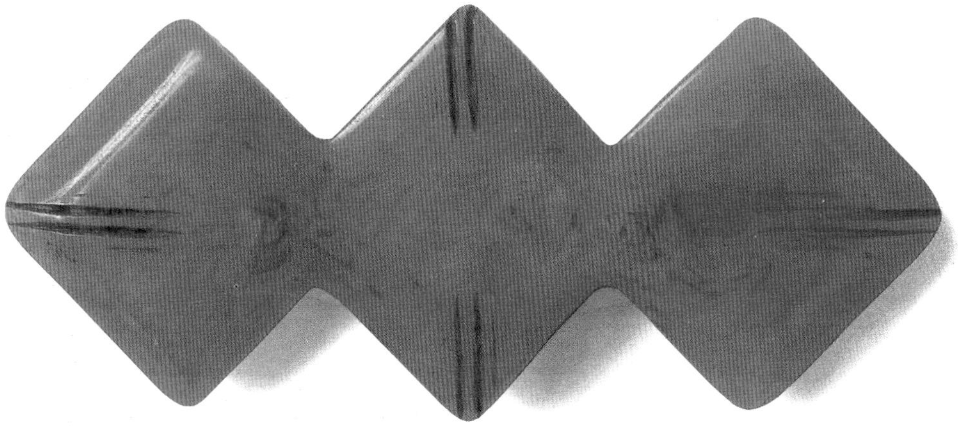

5 *A bar pin in the shape of a plain bow.*

6 *Bright red pin. It features a heavy-carved floral design.*

7 *Stylish bow pins. These were produced using a tracery mechanism.*

8 *Bow pins. The same design was often used on several different colors.*

9 *Carved bar pins. As they developed, the pins took on more complex designs. These show light to medium carving.*

9

10

10 *Clear and tortoiseshell bar pins. Light to medium carved, they are made from the side of a tube and not from flat stock.*

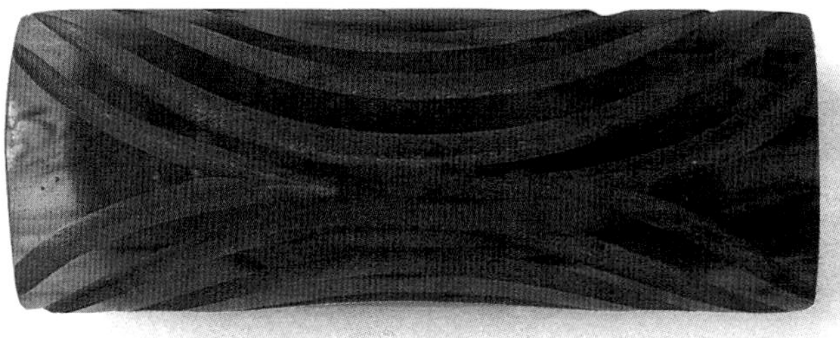

11 *Light-carved bar pins. These pieces came in all shapes and sizes.*

11

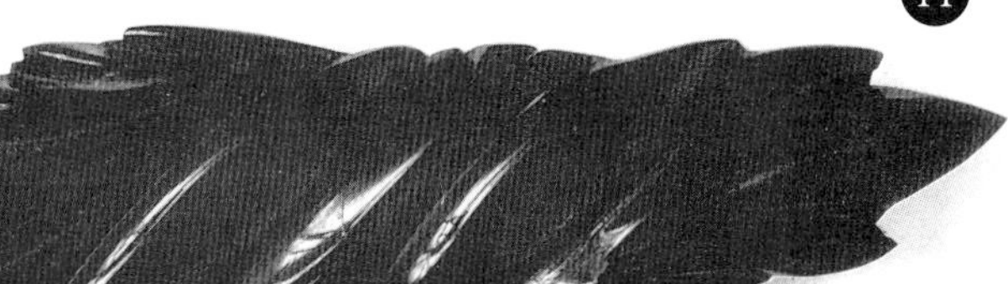

12 *Orange oval pin. It has a green laminated flower as center.*

13 *A large resin-washed flower pin.*

14 *Rose pin. Of European origin, it has a brass filigree frame.*

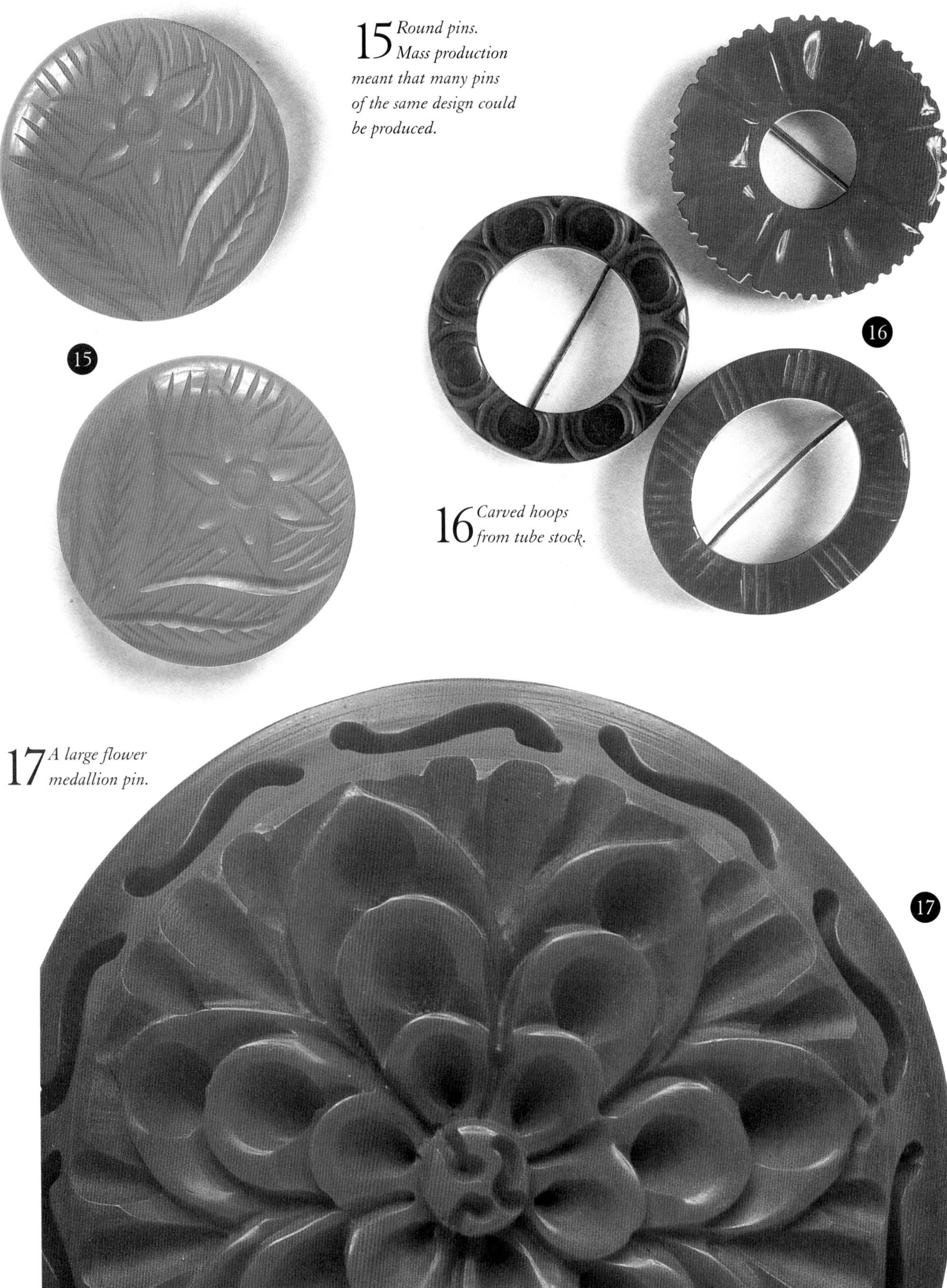

15 *Round pins. Mass production meant that many pins of the same design could be produced.*

16 *Carved hoops from tube stock.*

17 *A large flower medallion pin.*

18 *A tortoiseshell-colored floral pin.*

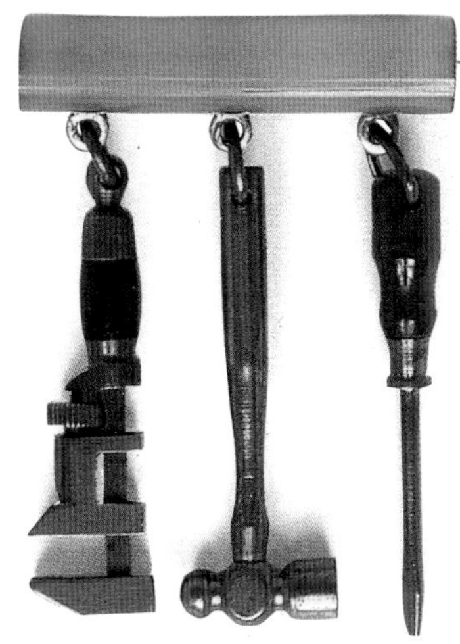

19 *Pin with actual working tools attached to the Catalin handle. It is possibly of German origin.*

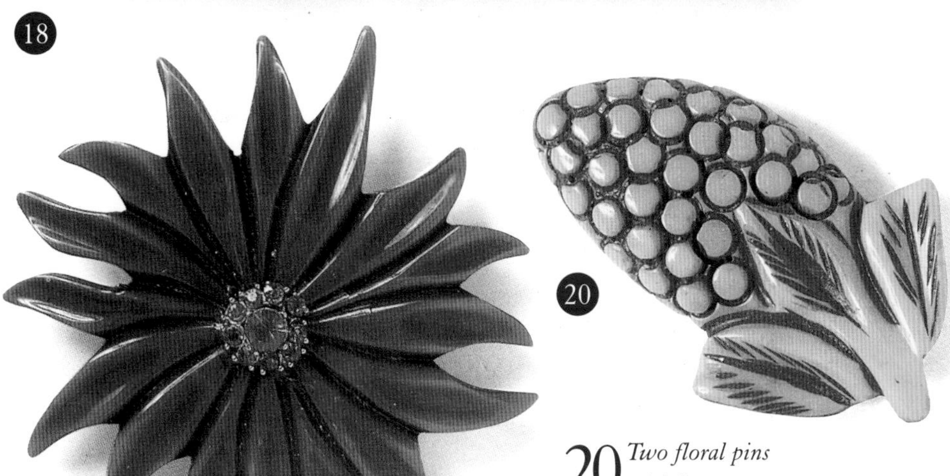

20 *Two floral pins with heavy carving.*

21 *Cobalt-colored floral pin. Possibly of German origin, it has brass trimmings.*

22 Classic angular pins. The design of these pieces was influenced by the Art Deco movement.

23 Simply-carved heart. This was originally white but has darkened through oxidation.

25 A hat-shaped pin based on a European theme.

24 Two stylish pins in the shape of a hat. The style is a reminder of the Art Deco era.

26 *Round pin. The "Speak no evil, see no evil, hear no evil" monkeys are on an orange-and-black laminated base.*

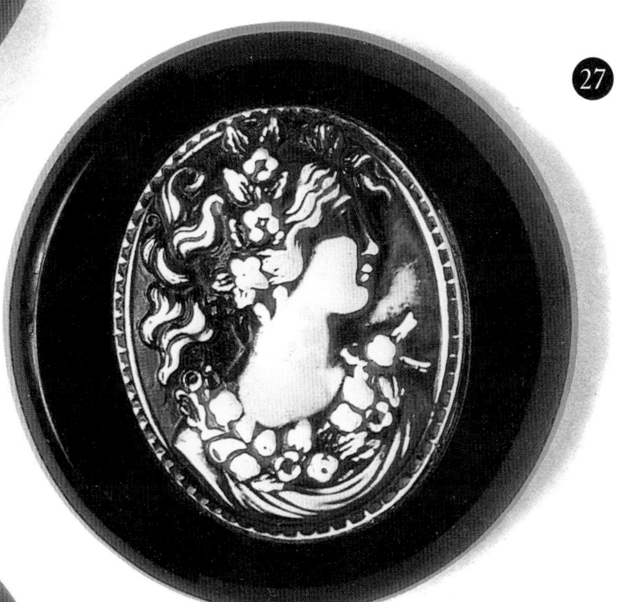

27 *A celluloid cameo on a white-and-black laminated base. This piece was influenced by the Victorian revival.*

28 *A celluloid cameo on a red-and-green laminated base. Like the piece in Fig. 27 it reflects the Victorian influence.*

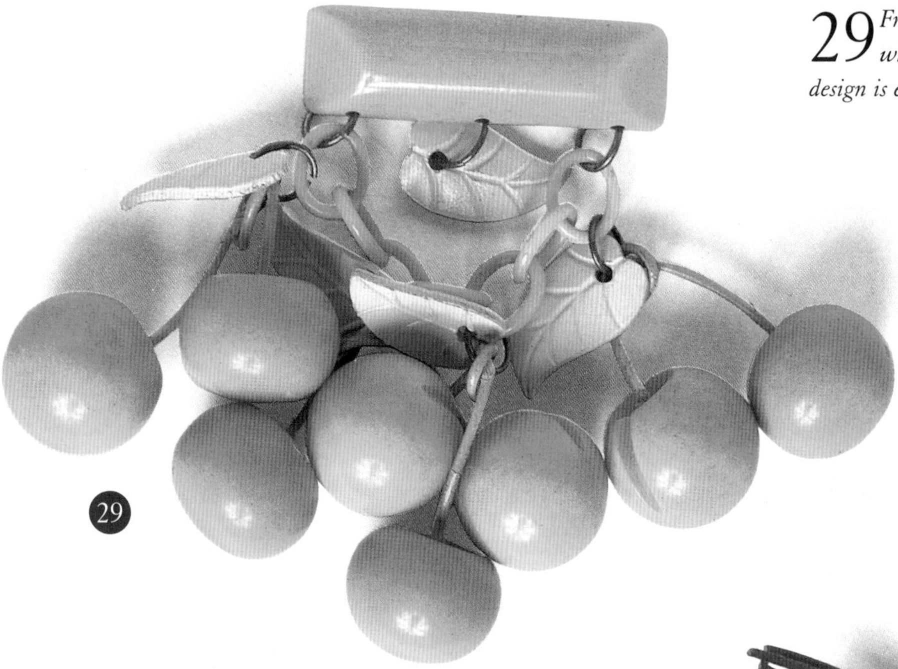

29 *Fruit pin. This white cherry design is extremely rare.*

29

30

30 *Heart pin with cherries.*

31

31 *Strawberry pin. Like the cherry piece (Fig. 29) it is very rare.*

32

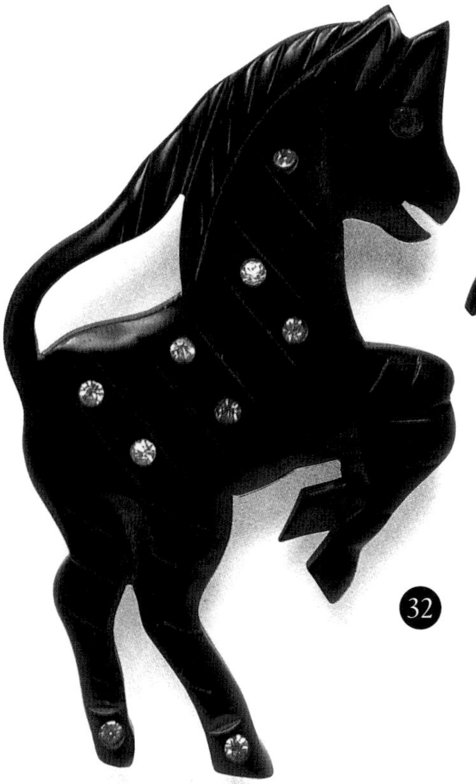

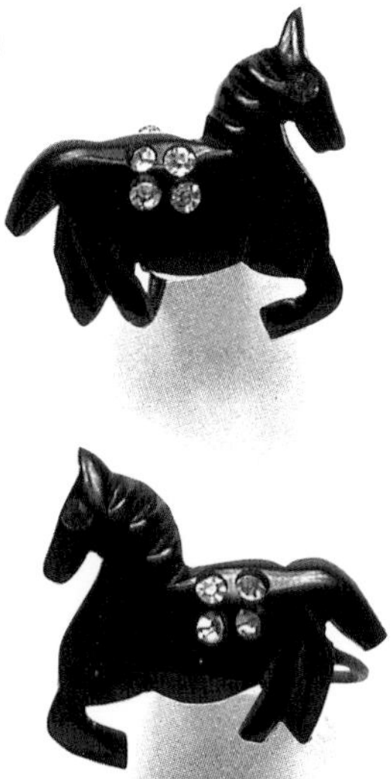

32 *Horse pin with matching earrings. This set is of European design.*

33

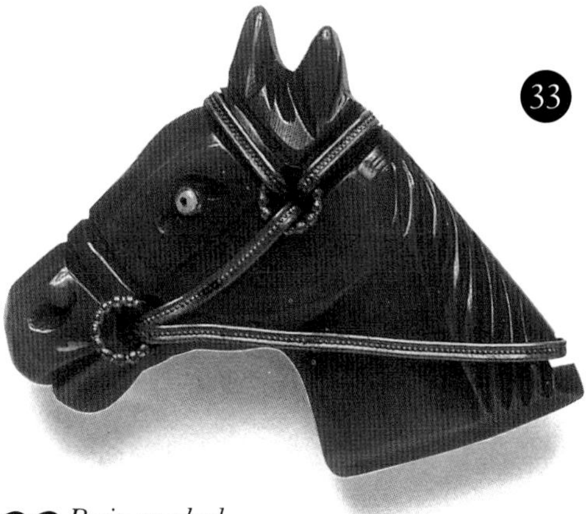

33 *Resin-washed horse's head pin. Animals formed a huge proportion of Bakelite pins.*

35

35 *Majestic resin-washed stallion with brass trimmings.*

34

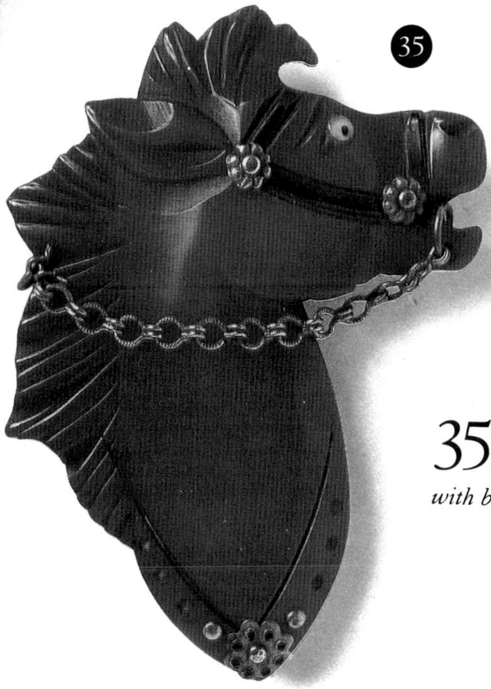

34 *Simple white horse pin. The piece has darkened through oxidation.*

36

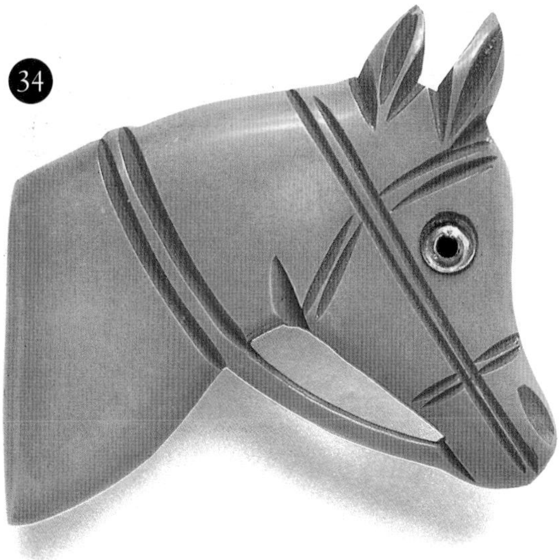

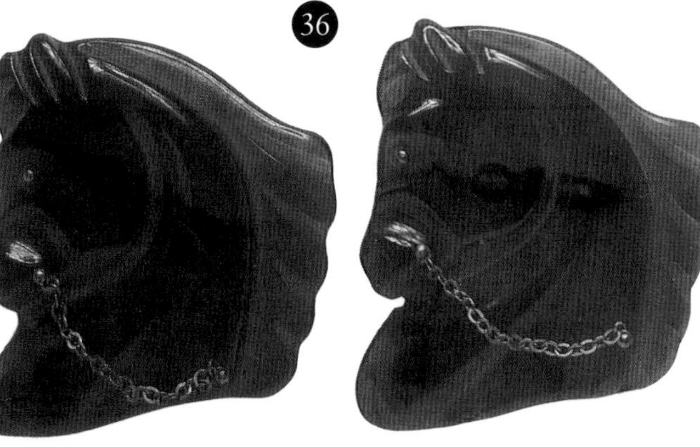

36 *Matching tortoiseshell-colored horse heads.*

37 *White walking Scottie.*

37

38 *Small triple Scottie pin.*

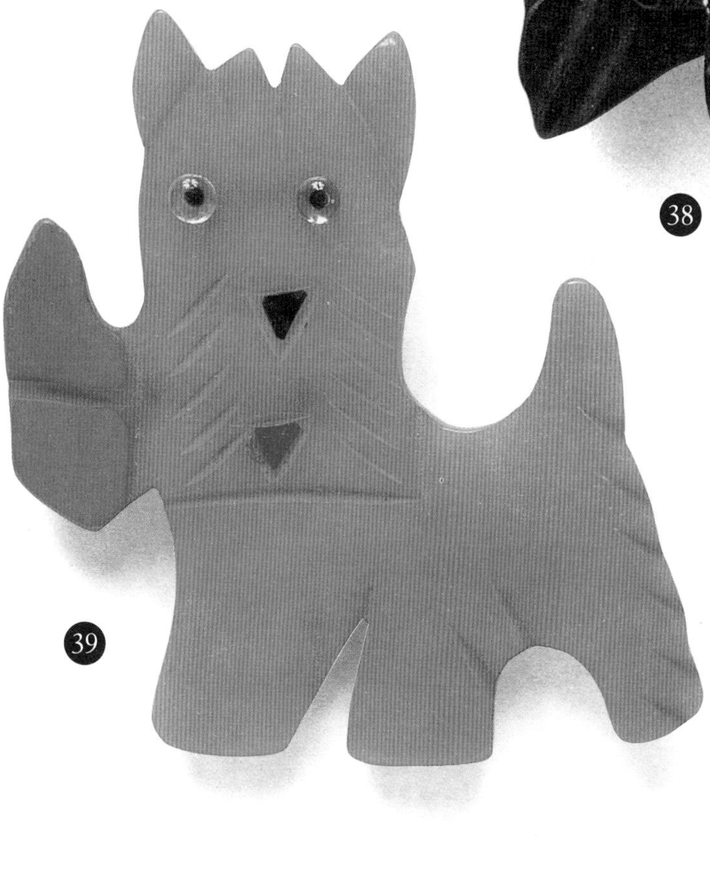

38

39

39 *Scottie dog with a painted bow. The Scottie became one of the most popular pin designs ever.*

40 *Simple animal shapes with painted highlights.*

41 *Plain animal shapes.*

42 *White animal on an acrylic base.*

43

43 *Elephants, including a pink, painted one.*

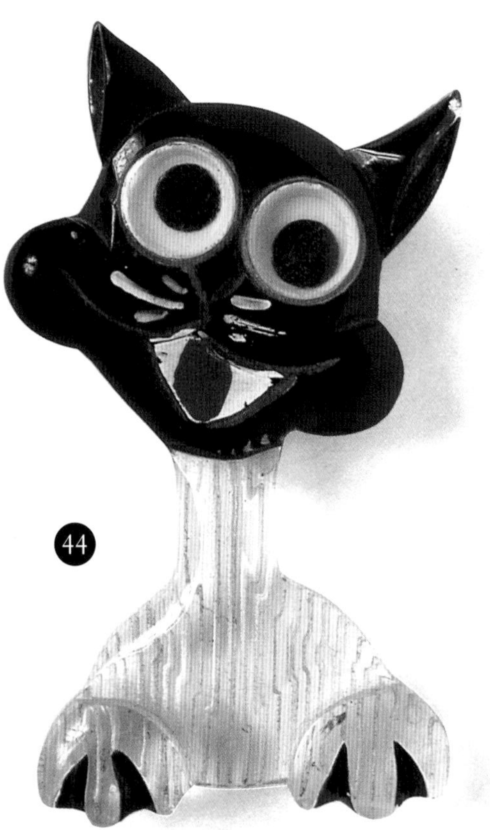

44 *Wacky cat. It has a Catalin head, acrylic body, and goggle eyes.*

45

45 *Cat pin. It has a brass body and Catalin legs.*

46 *Exotic bird. Of European origin, the base is chrome-plated metal, while the bird's body is clear Catalin.*

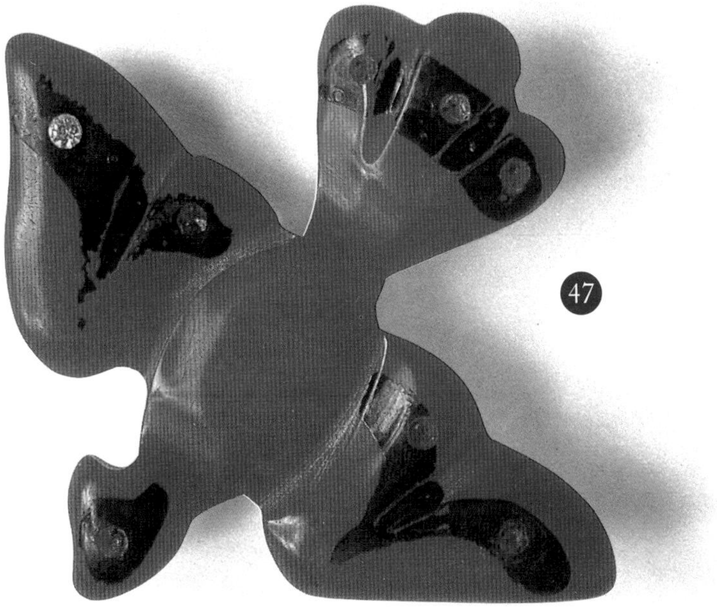

47 *Red bird. Made in France, it is decorated with paint and crystals.*

48 *Bird pins laminated on wood.*

49 *Pair of penguins. The black one is Catalin while the white one is made of urea. Birds were another recurring theme in pins.*

51 *Catalin bird with acrylic wings.*

50 *"Bird of Paradise," made from Catalin and acrylic.*

53 *Two bird pins.*

52 *White rooster with painted highlights.*

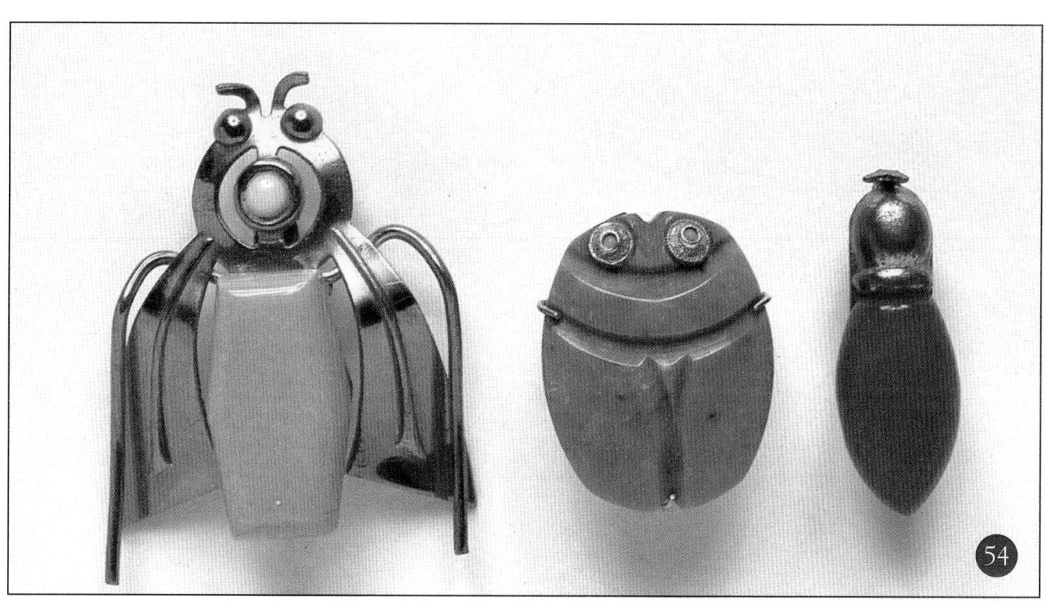

54 *A collection of bugs. Of European origin, they have Catalin bodies and brass trimmings.*

56 *A black bat over a butterscotch base. This was originally an assembly kit.*

55 *Simple butterfly shapes.*

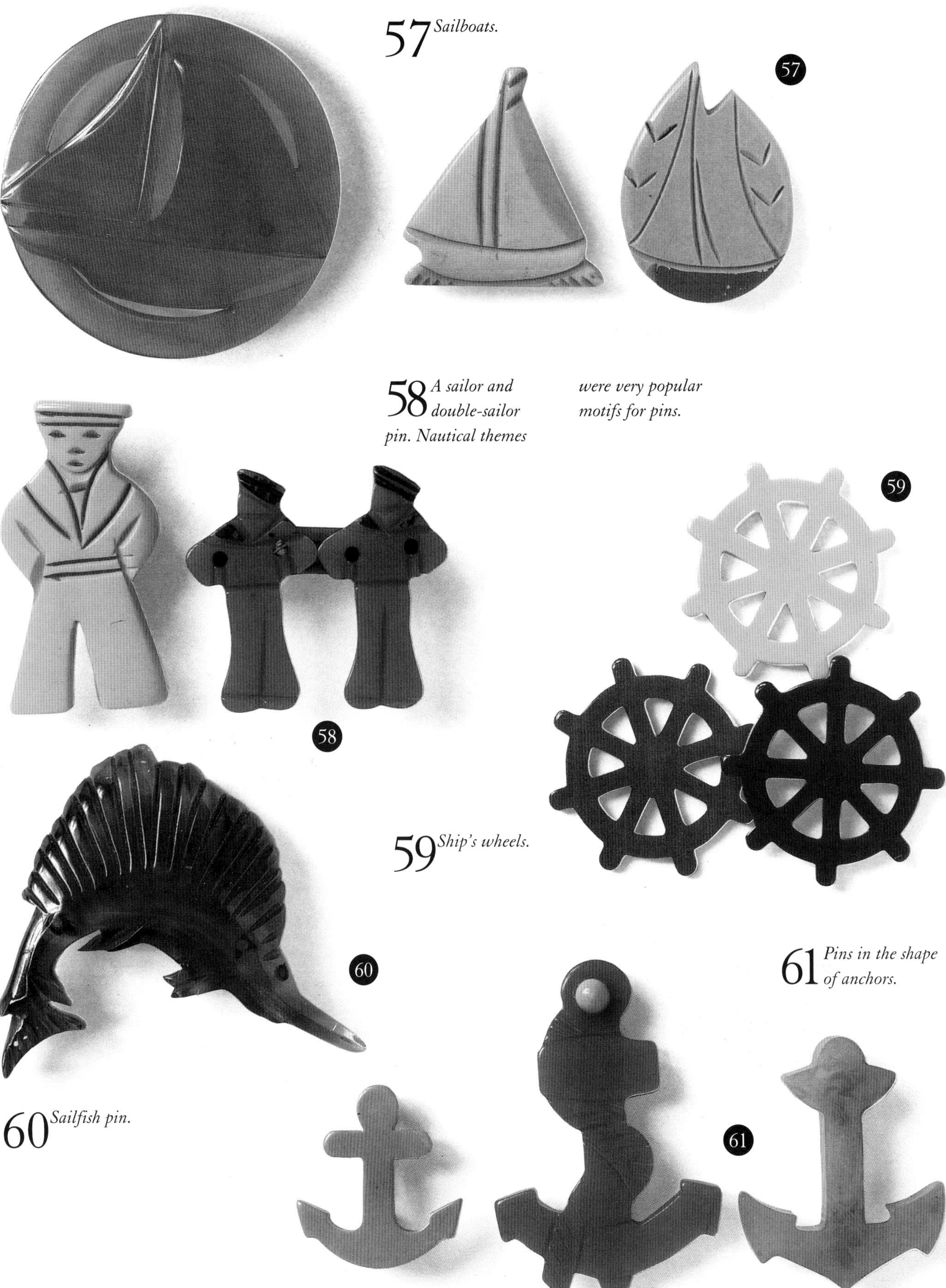

57 *Sailboats.*

58 *A sailor and double-sailor pin. Nautical themes were very popular motifs for pins.*

59 *Ship's wheels.*

60 *Sailfish pin.*

61 *Pins in the shape of anchors.*

Accessories

1 *A reticule. This smart little object would have been taken by a lady to a dance in the 1920s. It would contain rouge, powder, and, normally hidden behind the tassel, a lipstick. Rare and collectible, it is made of celluloid inset with paste. 1920s.*

2 *A fantastic belt made of Catalin links.*

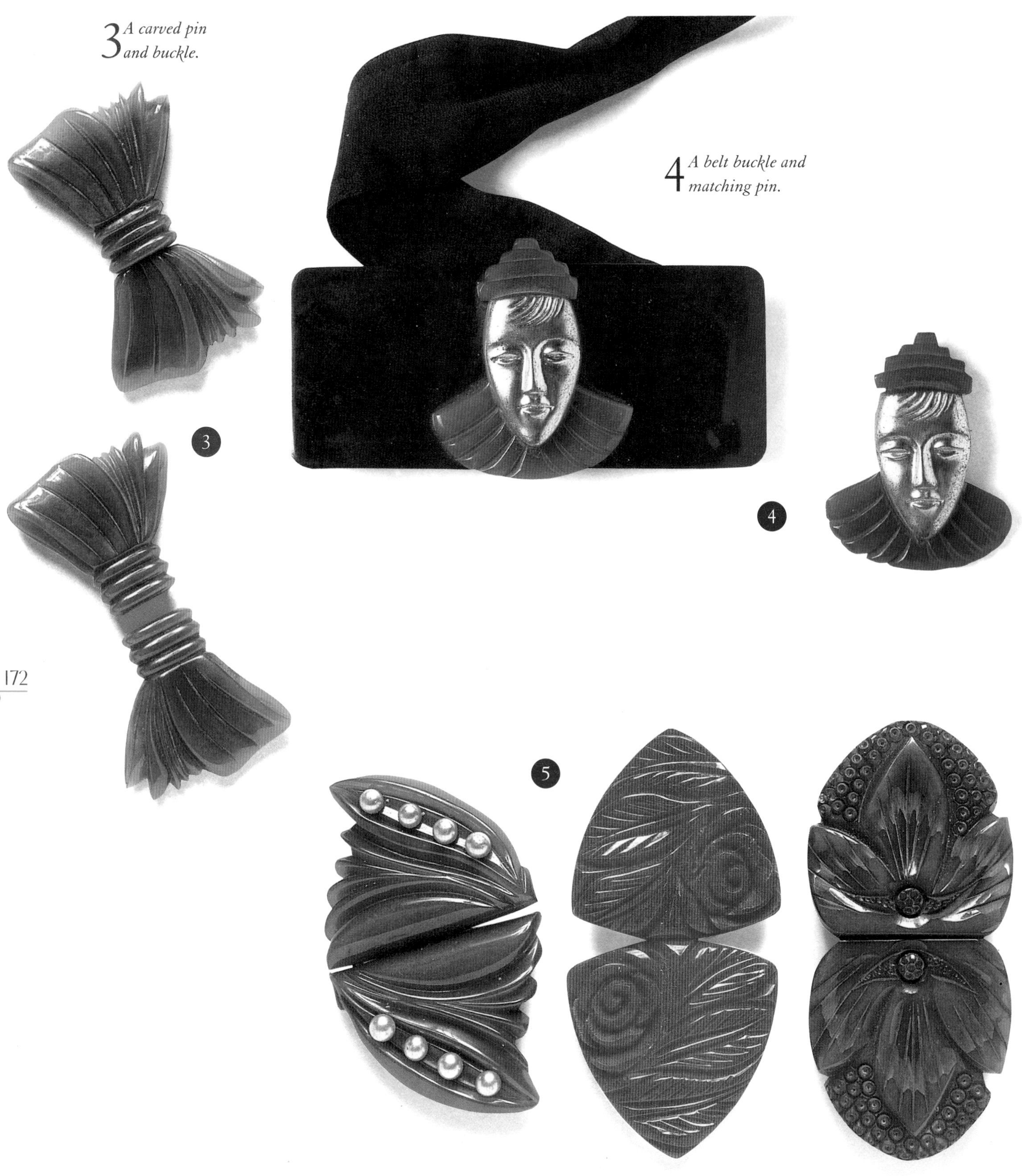

3 A carved pin and buckle.

4 A belt buckle and matching pin.

5 A pea-pod buckle (above left) and two carved buckles.

6 Cuff links and necktie clip. These were originally mistaken for amber.

7 "End of the day" umbrella handle.

8 A handbag and a clear Catalin frame.

Necklaces

Bakelite necklaces range from simple to attractively bizarre. Pendants, usually hung from either metal or celluloid, were probably the first neck pieces, with beading following close behind. As with other categories of jewelry metal signifies the European contribution, while the Americans found celluloid chain less expensive and easier to assemble.

There are many more beaded pieces than the more extensively carved or geometric designs. The beads were cut from cast cylinders and rounded according to the shape of the designer's needs. Some were rounded and others were oval-shaped. Any carving was done at this point. There are examples of faceting, as well as floral carvings. When the carving was finished they were tumbled to a finely polished finish. The drilling was the last thing to be done, in a machine which had a drill on each side, and the holes were drilled to each other. The holes vary according to the material used to link them together. This was mainly cotton thread but unfortunately it rotted over the years and many pieces have had to be restrung.

Some of the European productions were strung on chain or were affixed to metal findings. American neckwear seemed

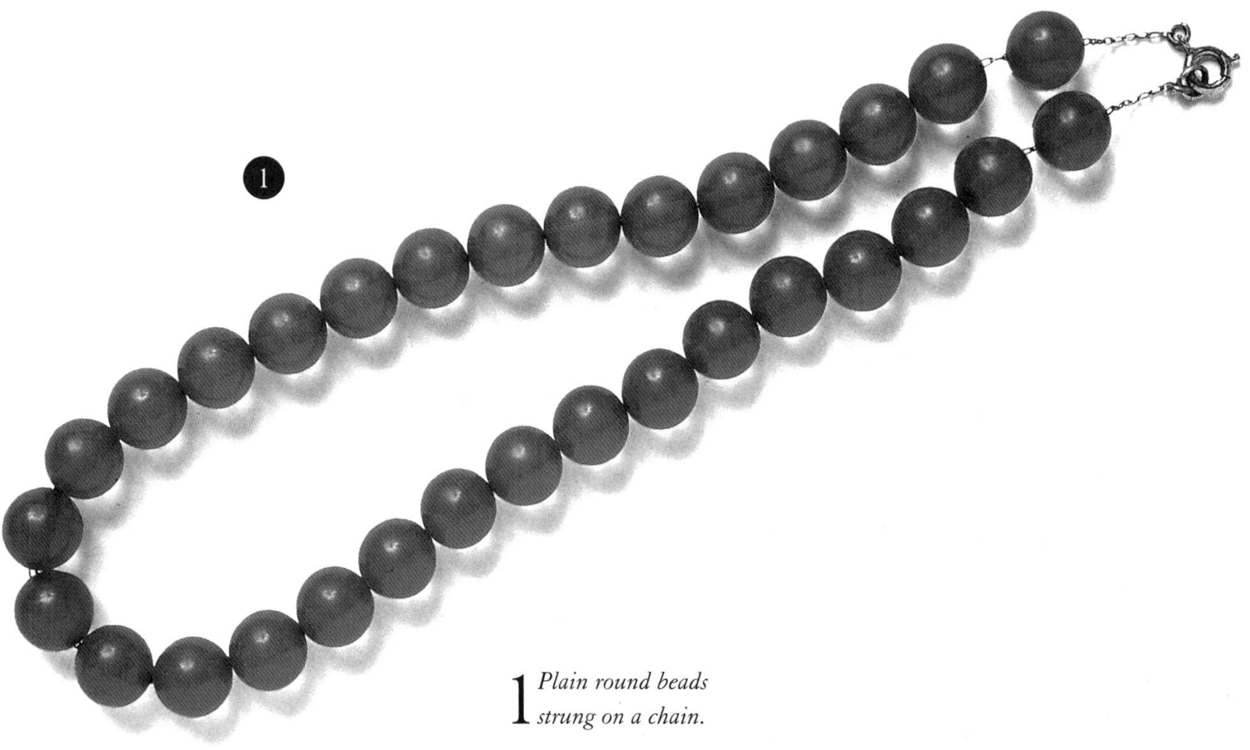

1 *Plain round beads strung on a chain.*

to be fashioned to keep away the blues. More boisterous than other designers, Americans had visions of fun stuff. The fruit and vegetable style carried over into neckwear completing sets that had started with bracelets. There are, of course, exceptions to every rule but this seems to be the norm. Two such exceptions are the geometric necklaces that were produced in the States and the fun "tool" necklaces from Germany.

Both continents touched on Victorian revival, and the Americans embraced the fluid and then the mechanical styles of the Art Deco era.

2 Geometric design with multicolored half-disks.

2

3

3 Very long, flapper-type clear necklace, simulating amber.

4 Stick necklace. The chain is celluloid.

5 Elongated beads that simulate amber.

6 *Jagged rustic necklace of geometric design.*

6

8

7 *Simulated tortoiseshell necklace. The chain is celluloid.*

8 *Necklace, earrings, and bracelet with metal findings. All are part of a set of Catalin eggs, possibly of European origin.*

7

9 *A great necklace of carved white leaves over brass findings. It is probably of European origin.*

10 *Cherry necklace. The chain is brass.*

11 *Cherry necklace with matching pin. The chains are celluloid and the cherries are carved Catalin.*

12 *A neckplate piece hung on a chain.*

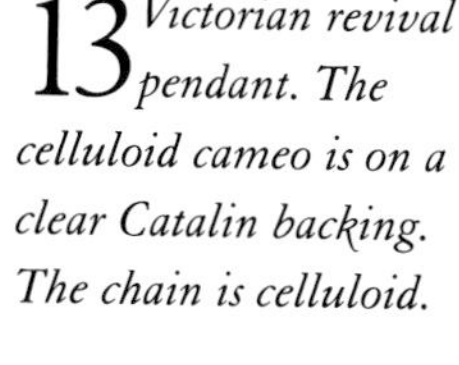

13 *Victorian revival pendant. The celluloid cameo is on a clear Catalin backing. The chain is celluloid.*

14 *Carved white roses are combined with black round beads.*

Rings and earrings

Rings were made in the customary design of other pieces of jewelry but over the years many have been lost and they are therefore difficult to locate. Prison rings, however, are more abundant. They were fabricated in different prisons, mainly in the United States. The bulk of these rings have men's pictures in them, and seem to have a very small band. A few are larger: one with a baby's picture, and another with a picture of a woman, probably made by an inmate for his own wearing. Another shows a man with a dog; this is also in a man's size, but most of the rings were probably made for a wife, girlfriend, or other loved one as a remembrance of the individual who was in prison.

They were made from all sorts of things. Bakelite being the most accessible plastic of the era, the creative inmate could salvage the end of his toothbrush or the bottom of his shaving brush. A slice off a Bakelite fountain pen made a great band on which to build the ring. In the North Carolina State Penitentiary inmates who participated in recreation periods used this time to make jewelry. Adhesives were less accessible than a match and a piece of celluloid, so the ringmaker used celluloid because it was flammable and used it to bond the layers of the more intricate laminated pieces.

There are rings that conform to the geometric style, both in stripes and polka dots, and also angular-type pieces as well as ones with traditional floral motifs. Bakelite earrings are much more plentiful and can be worn by themselves or to complement a necklace that has been fashioned to the same design. They come with all kinds of different findings—clips, screw backs, and the less common pierced backs. Some of the earrings lend themselves to signatures, so it is more common to find a pair of signed earrings than, say, a bangle.

The earring can be funky in itself: a huge piece in a floral design, for example, or several beads strung down almost to shoulder-length. Some are simply balls cut in half.

Earrings were generally part of a parure, so they come in the usual geometrics.

Rings

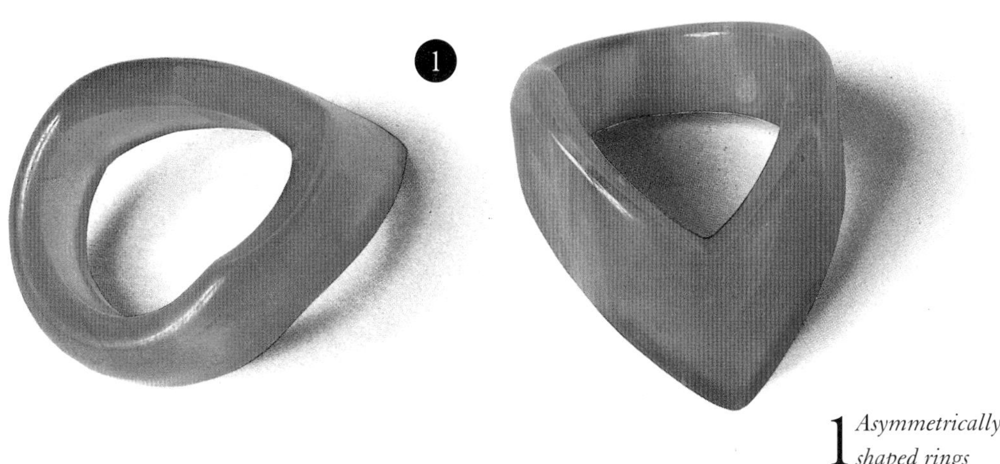

1 *Asymmetrically shaped rings*

2 *Striped rings.*

3 *Fun rings in different shapes.*

Earrings

1 *Clip-on and screw-back earrings. These were more prominent than ones for pierced ears.*

2 *Hoop earrings for pierced ears.*

3 Dangling earrings. They were probably the final addition to a set, complementing the necklace, bangle, and pin.

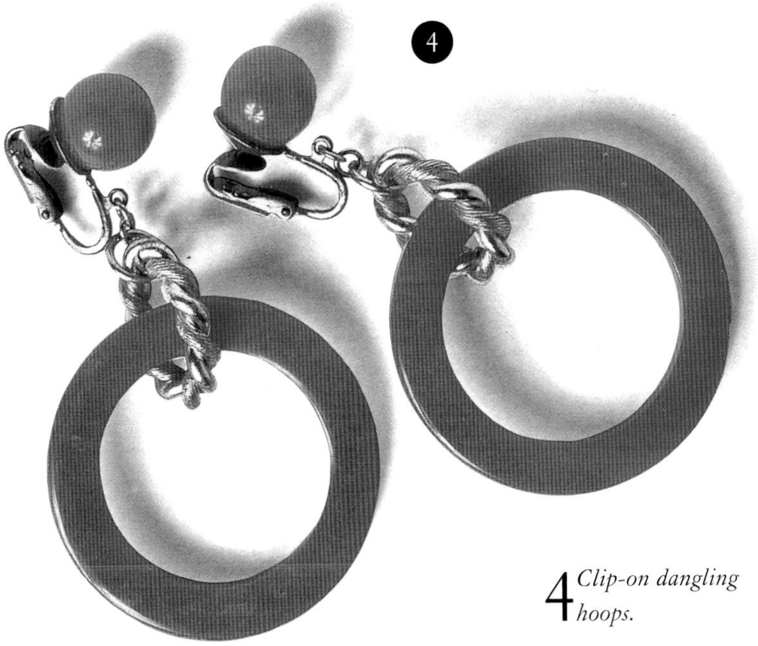

3

4

4 Clip-on dangling hoops.

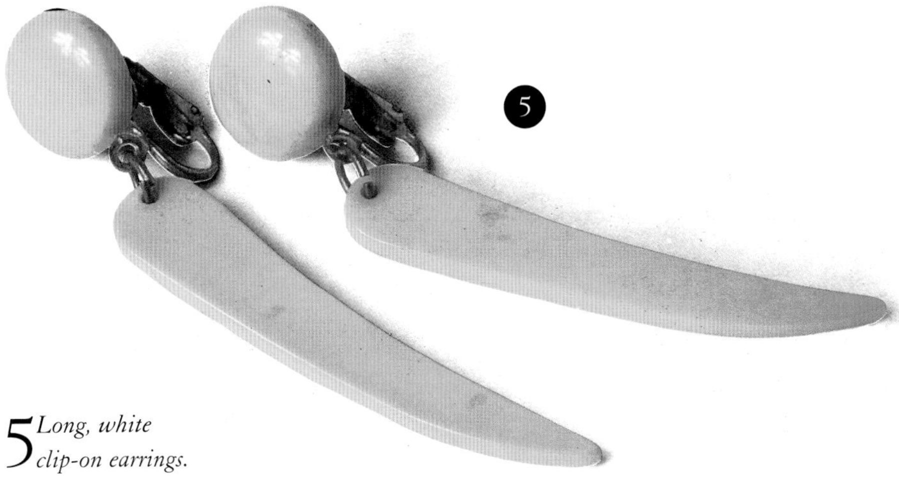

5

5 Long, white clip-on earrings.

6 *Clear carved earrings. One pair is of Art Deco design, the other floral.*

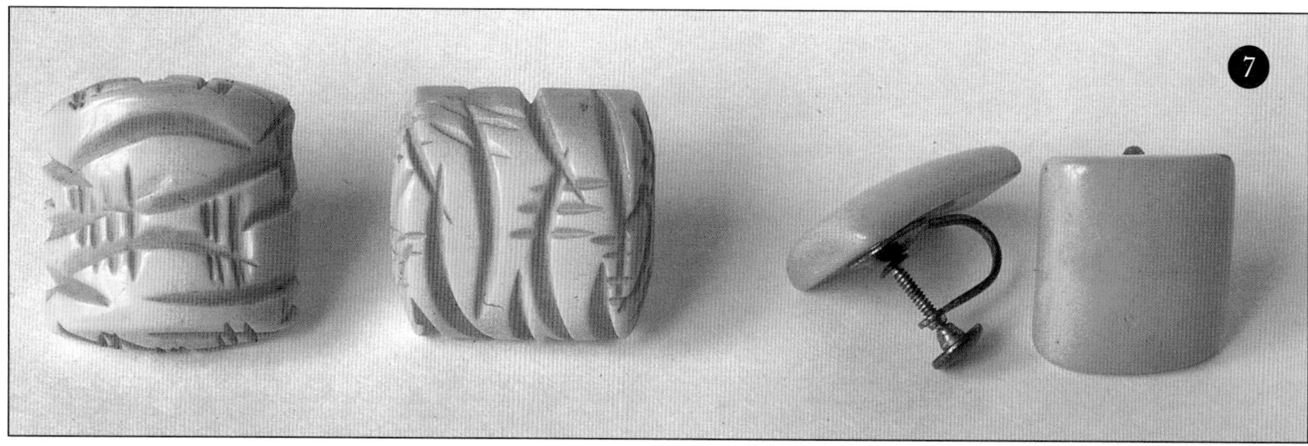

7 *Two pairs of white squares. One is carved and the other plain.*

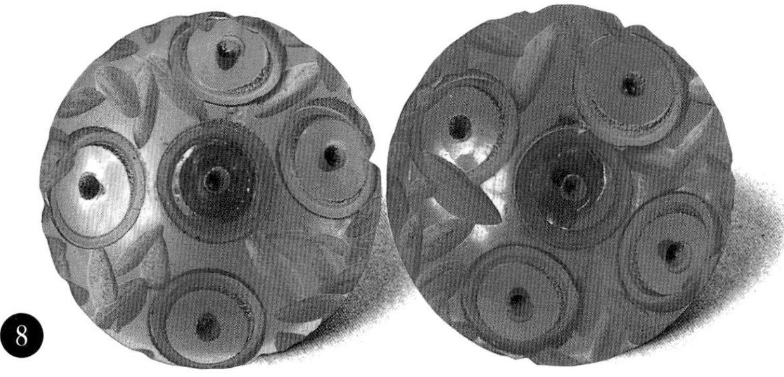

8 *Small, round, clear, and carved earrings. These are for pierced ears.*

9 *A pair of heavy-carved leaf clip-ons.*

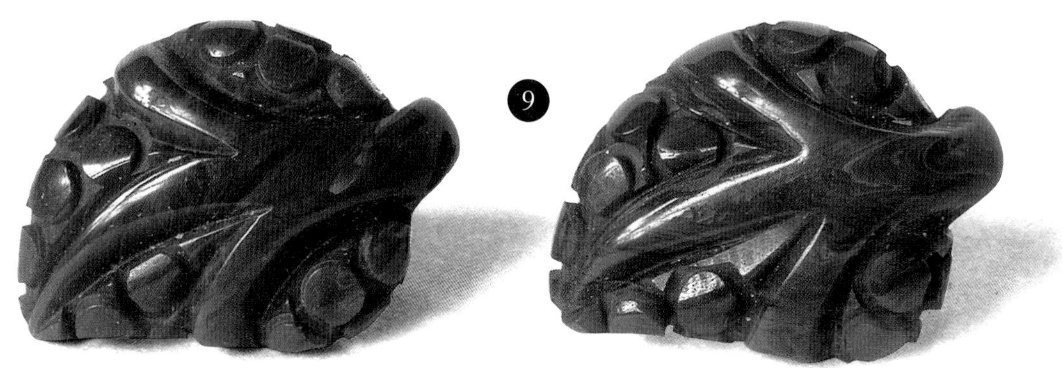

10 *Very large, heavy-carved, cobalt-colored earrings. These are for pierced ears.*

11 *A pair of oriental faces.*

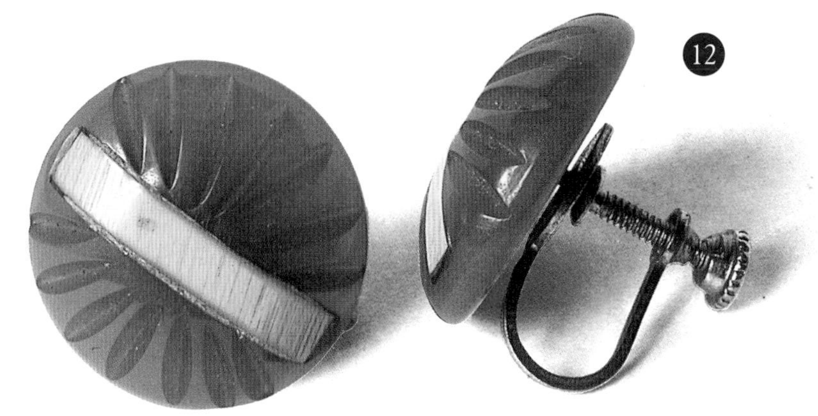

12 *Striped, screw-back earring, with carving.*

Plastics and color

However versatile it was in other respects, Bakelite's color range, compared to that of later plastics, was acknowledged to be limited. This limited range was due to several factors. In principle, the brightest and purest hues are generally obtained by adding color to a colorless material but phenol-formaldehyde had a "self color" which affected the final result. Most dark colors such as browns, reds, ochers, greens, and black remained untainted, but light colors and blue and purple were particularly difficult to achieve. Another constraint was the instability of the material when affected by heat, light, or aging. Phenol-formaldehyde gradually assumes a dark yellow hue under intense heat and thus cast-phenolic objects in particular experience a color change over a period of time, particularly if exposed to the sun's rays. Creamy white turns nicotine yellow, and both blue and violet may take on a greenish cast.

The decline in popularity of Bakelite, which occurred after World War II, was brought about in part by its reputation for "dull" colors. The public grew weary of the somber tones imposed during the thirties, leading to an inevitable demand for brighter colors. This was met by the development of urea-formaldehyde, created by substituting urea (ammonia and carbon dioxide) in place of phenol, to obtain a thermosetting molding powder similar in all respects to Bakelite, but with greater color possibilities. Unlike self-colored phenol-formaldehyde, the basic

Translucent burgundy pin, bangle, and earrings with the same carving on all the pieces.

urea resin is transparent and light-fast — thus all colors and hues, including blues, pastels, and pure white, could be easily created, with a high degree of permanency. Urea-formaldehyde came to be known as "Beetleware" or simply "Beatl" and displayed several variations on the plain color range. The addition of fillers such as bleached paper pulp resulted in the characteristic mottled effect which became the trademark of British manufacturers Brookes and Adams with their Bandalastaware products, which included picnic sets, lamps, boxes, and candlesticks. Although urea moldings are lighter in weight than phenolics, urea has less resistance to water and could be prone to warping or buckling. Use of urea moldings was largely confined to items such as tableware—unlike Bakelite, which more than lived up to its billing as "the material of a thousand uses."

This fruit bowl by Brookes & Adams was made from thiourea-formaldehyde or Beatl in 1929. Bandalastaware was first exhibited at the 1925 Wembley Fair, London, with great success. The purity of the colors and the translucency of the material made for the unusual marbled effects and the appearance of stony solidity. In 1929, the Beetle shop (named after the material) opened in Regent Street, London, to a throng of curious customers.

eugène

Business and industry

The design of industrial products, unlike later consumer goods, was determined in the main by their function. Bakelite was valued for its electrical insulation properties in switches and plugs, and as a tough engineering material. It could be easily machined and accept a heavy mechanical load. Unlike natural materials, Bakelite plastics were manmade and could be manufactured within the laboratory to suit specific demands. In its various forms, Bakelite was eagerly adapted to the growing needs of industry. Bakelite molding materials of various grades became widely used—as a thermosetting plastic it had the virtue of being resistant to heat, moisture, and chemicals. Bakelite adhesives (in the form of liquid cement) increased efficiency when used to make grinding wheels for machines and brake linings for the automobile industry. Hot- and cold-setting adhesives (consisting of phenolic or urea resins) were also used to make furniture and plywood. Bakelite lacquers had highly developed anticorrosive properties and, as a result, were used in varnishes and enamels to increase their durability.

One product in particular, Bakelite Laminated, proved especially versatile over a wide range of electrical and engineering applications. Strong enough to be machined, and an all-purpose lightweight insulator, it was made by impregnating a base material (fabric or paper) with a synthetic resin. Sheets were then bonded together under heat and pressure to form a laminated composite approximately one-sixteenth of an inch thick. The resulting sheet was tough, dimensionally stable, and very versatile. Transport systems which relied on the supply of electricity—electric trains, trolley buses, and tramways—used Bakelite Laminated for its insulating properties and durability. Bakelite Laminated was employed for terminal panels, flash barriers in transformers, and the insulation of relay sets. Bakelite molding material was also used for instrument housing, sequence circuit switches, control knobs, fuse carriers, and numerous nonelectrical applications, such as the cooling blade fan.

Laminated plastics had other transport-related functions. Luxury ocean liners such as the *Queen Mary* and the *Queen Elizabeth* were equipped with durable, wipe-clean surfaces made from Warerite (a subsidiary of Bakelite), which supplied wall paneling, flush doors and bar and counter surfaces in a range of colors. Formica, Roanoid and Micarta were the later plastic laminates of the forties and fifties.

One of Bakelite Laminated's more unusual industrial applications was to aid metal detection. It was employed by food manufacturers to eliminate stray particles of metal that might contaminate end products. Yet again it was Bakelite Laminated's mechanical strength and insulating properties which led to its use inside the search head of the metal detector. No doubt as a precaution, the oscillator coils of the detector were impregnated with Bakelite varnish.

Bakelite also had many uses in the workshop. Although never likely to replace metal, it could be machined to make precision tools and was frequently used in the fabrication of jigs for drilling and welding, gluing, and assembly fixtures. The jigs were strong, lightweight, and could be quickly and cheaply machined in the workshop when required.

Industrial design

During the thirties, the rise of the plastics industry was inextricably bound up with the development of the new profession of industrial design. The founding fathers of industrial design in America—Raymond Loewy, Harold Van Doren, Norman Bel Geddes, Henry Dreyfuss, and Walter Dorwin Teague—had varying backgrounds (commercial art, advertising, stage design), but all were linked by a keen graphic sense and a strong element of showmanship. They were lured to industry in order to redesign and restyle products with the aim of giving them added "sales appeal" in the competitive and floundering Depression economy.

1 "A profusion of plastics for domestic and personal use is shown here to colorful advantage." Thus reads a caption in a magazine article on plastics in the home. Note the highly desirable Round Ekco Bakelite radio in the background.

Industrial designers generally worked as consultants to several firms at the same time, applying their skills to a diverse range of products. As Raymond Loewy put it, "Everything from a lipstick to a locomotive." Most insisted on developing a close working relationship with engineers, so as to understand better the processes of manufacture which had such a crucial bearing on the final design. However, on a purely commercial level, their primary task was to produce an eye-catching package that would help to boost sales.

Despite these efforts, there was still a lingering fear on the part of the industry that the public might reject plastics as an inferior substitute. This gave rise to an aggressive campaign to suggest that synthetic materials had exactly the qualities required to meet the challenge of the future. The Bakelite Corporation led the way in convincing manufacturers to beautify products with plastic. In 1932 the firm held a symposium to acquaint designers with the technical advantages and limitations of Bakelite as a material as well as its stylistic potential. During the next two years, the trade magazines *Modern Plastics* and *Sales Management* ran a series of advertisements focusing on industrial designers and the creative way in which they made use of

Bakelite. Each advertisement concentrated on a single product, together with a small photograph and potted biography touting the designer as a celebrity and his views on modern design. *Modern Plastics* of June 1934 featured the ubiquitous Raymond Loewy and a radically restyled duplicating machine. "Raymond Loewy says, 'The New Deal in industrial design is establishing the triumph of beauty through simplicity' . . . " ran the banner headline. The copy continued: "That 'Manufacturers have discovered the buying public's inherent taste for simple beauty and its appreciation of fundamentally good lines' is a contention of Mr Loewy's. Of invaluable help to the designer in his search for simple, beautiful lines are Bakelite Materials."

The products selected for these advertisements ranged from utilitarian objects such as knobs and handles, to personal accessories like barometers and telephone indexes. Domestic items such as irons and washing machines were contrasted with business equipment. Throughout ran the powerful underlying message that Bakelite—"The material of a thousand uses" — would revitalize industry and reshape the environment.

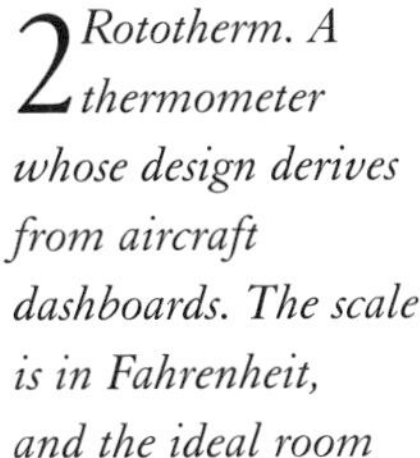

2 Rototherm. A thermometer whose design derives from aircraft dashboards. The scale is in Fahrenheit, and the ideal room temperature or "comfort zone" seems to have been between 60 and 70 degrees. Made of urea-formaldehyde. Late 1940s.

4 Davenset volt meter. This battery tester, with its pistol grip, would not be out of place as a ray gun in a Buck Rogers movie. The two antenna-type contact points would have been placed on the terminals of a suspect battery. Bakelite. 1947.

3 Morse telegraph key. A purely functional boxy design. Bakelite. 1940s.

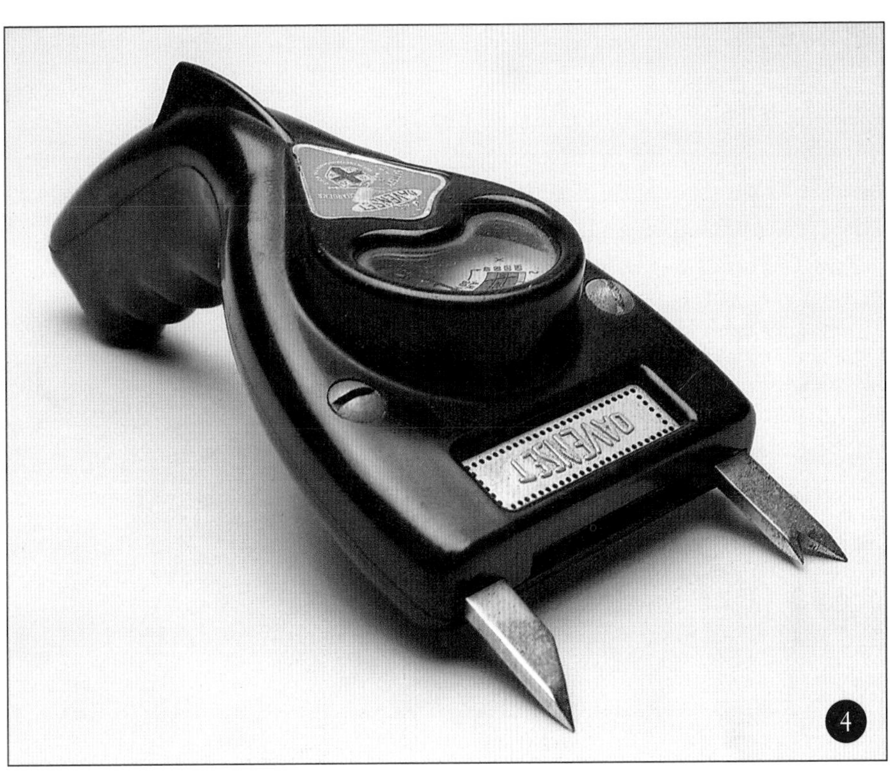

Office equipment

1 Bates index, designed by Norman Bel Geddes for Bates Manufacturing Co. Ltd. This innovative design with a streamlined influence curiously missed out the letters FIJPQX and Y. Evidently fewer clients' names began with these characters! Bakelite. 1925.

2 Esterbrook dip-less fountain well. This highly elegant double teardrop-shaped design is a good example of the mannerisms of streamlining applied in a nonfunctional way. Bakelite. 1930s.

3 Carvacraft pen holder and blotter, "A Dickinson Product." Two of a vast range of desk accessories exhibiting Art Deco styling of a striking purity for such a late date. Cast-phenolic resin. 1948.

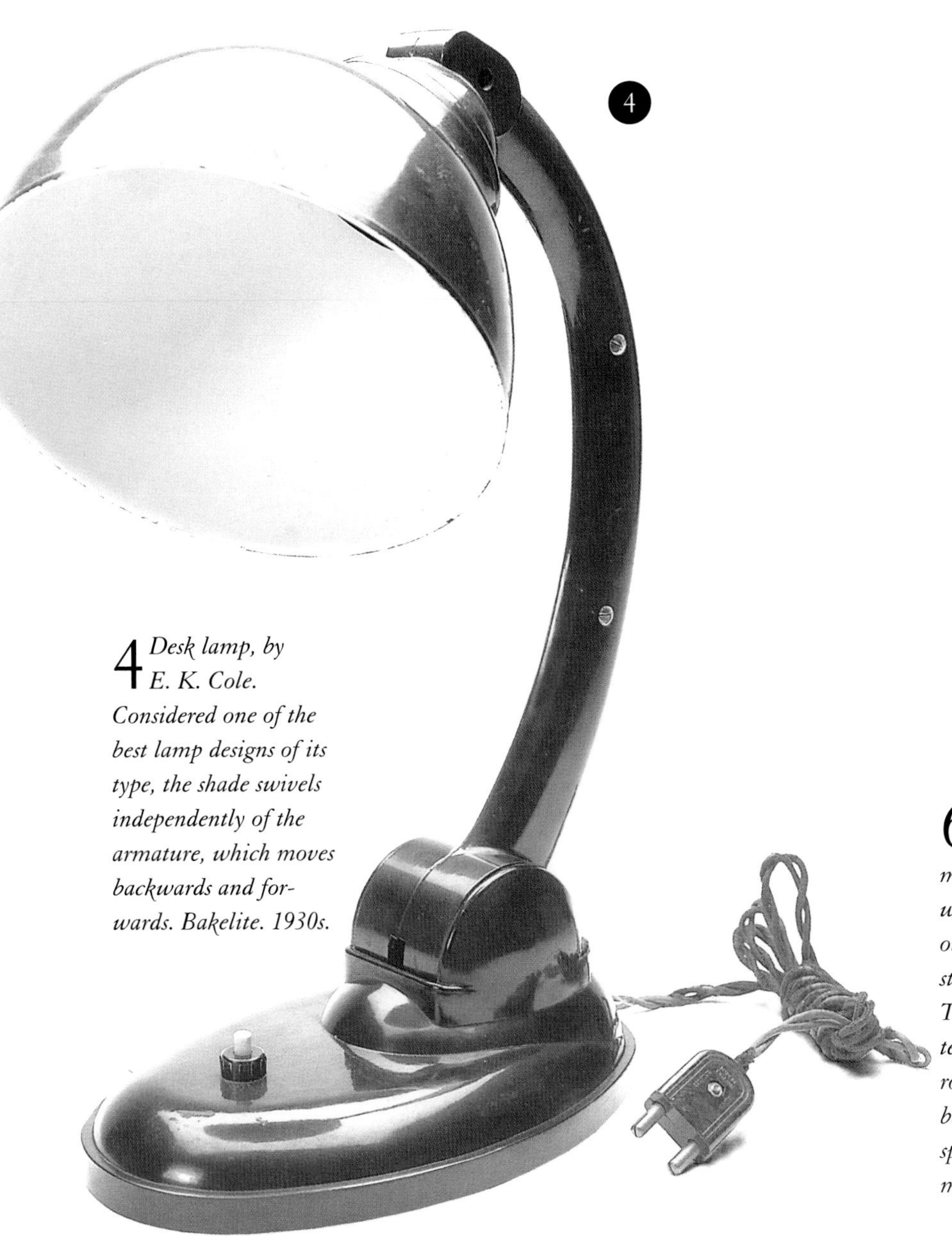

4 *Desk lamp, by E. K. Cole. Considered one of the best lamp designs of its type, the shade swivels independently of the armature, which moves backwards and forwards. Bakelite. 1930s.*

6 *Desk-top microphone. A microphone that wouldn't have been out of place in a BBC studio of the 1930s. The chromium telescopic stand is rooted in a Bakelite base; the floating spring microphone is made of casein. 1936.*

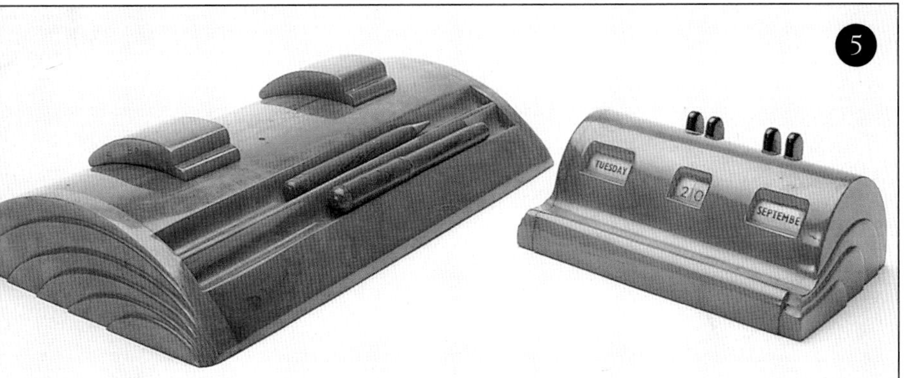

5 *Carvacraft double inkwell and push button calendar, "A Dickinson Product." The twin fitted caps slide back to reveal one black and one red inkwell. The calendar is extremely rare and very attractively styled. The range was produced in three colors: yellow, amber, and green. Cast-phenolic resin. 1948.*

Streamlining and cleanlining

A symbiotic relationship gradually developed between the plastics industry and industrial design. The ideological thrust of Modernism stressed the importance of new materials such as plastic and, in turn, plastic became firmly associated with the ideals and spread of modern design. Furthermore, the most economical ways of designing molds for the manufacture of plastic products proved ideally suited to the new Machine Age styles. Designs could be cut into a mold by machine tools, thus eliminating the expense of hand labor. This method favored simple, modern forms and in particular an aerodynamic style of design known as "streamlining," which flourished in America during the thirties.

The streamlined style originally arose out of scientific research into the perfect aerodynamic form. Since the late nineteenth century, scientists and engineers had been experimenting with the adaptation of organic forms to moving objects, with the aim of increasing speed and efficiency by offering the minimum resistance to wind and water. In 1938, the 20th Century Limited, the high-speed train that ran between New York and Chicago became the first "streamliner" to be put into commercial operation. Designed by Henry Dreyfuss, the smooth, bullet-shaped front of the engine was quite unlike existing trains, with no obvious protrusions such as funnels or pipes. Three years previously, the Douglas DC3 became the first streamlined aerodynamic airplane to use modern aluminum alloys in its lightweight construction. Streamlining quickly came to symbolize the aspirations of the new Machine Age. Low, sculptural, and flowing, streamlined design reflected American desire for a frictionless flight into the future.

Streamlining as applied to moving vehicles had obvious technological advantages—increased speed, more efficient fuel consumption, and added stability—but paradoxically its influence was equally great on a huge range of static consumer goods. Corporations quickly found that they were able to reflect the modern world through the streamlined nature of their products. Industrial designers recognized a dynamic beauty in the flowing, graceful lines and began to apply the streamlined aesthetic to a wide range of objects. Walter Dorwin Teague went so far as to call streamlining "characteristic of our age" and noted that it "expresses force and grace in whatever form it defines . . . there is surely no more exciting form in modern design." The positive associations of speed and efficiency were conveyed through numerous unrelated forms such as the wireless, refrigerator, iron, and television.

The shaver was a potent example of small-scale streamlining. Inventor of the "to and fro" system, Schick was first to introduce America to the electric shaver in 1931. It was a dry shave, unlike earlier electric shavers which still required the use of soap. Bakelite was chosen to house the shaving mechanism because of its insulating qualities and malleable, lightweight form. The Schick shaver had a black phenolic casing and in the first year alone several thousand men rushed out and willingly paid $25. Five years on, prices had dropped and the market had swelled to over a million, with new competition from Remington and

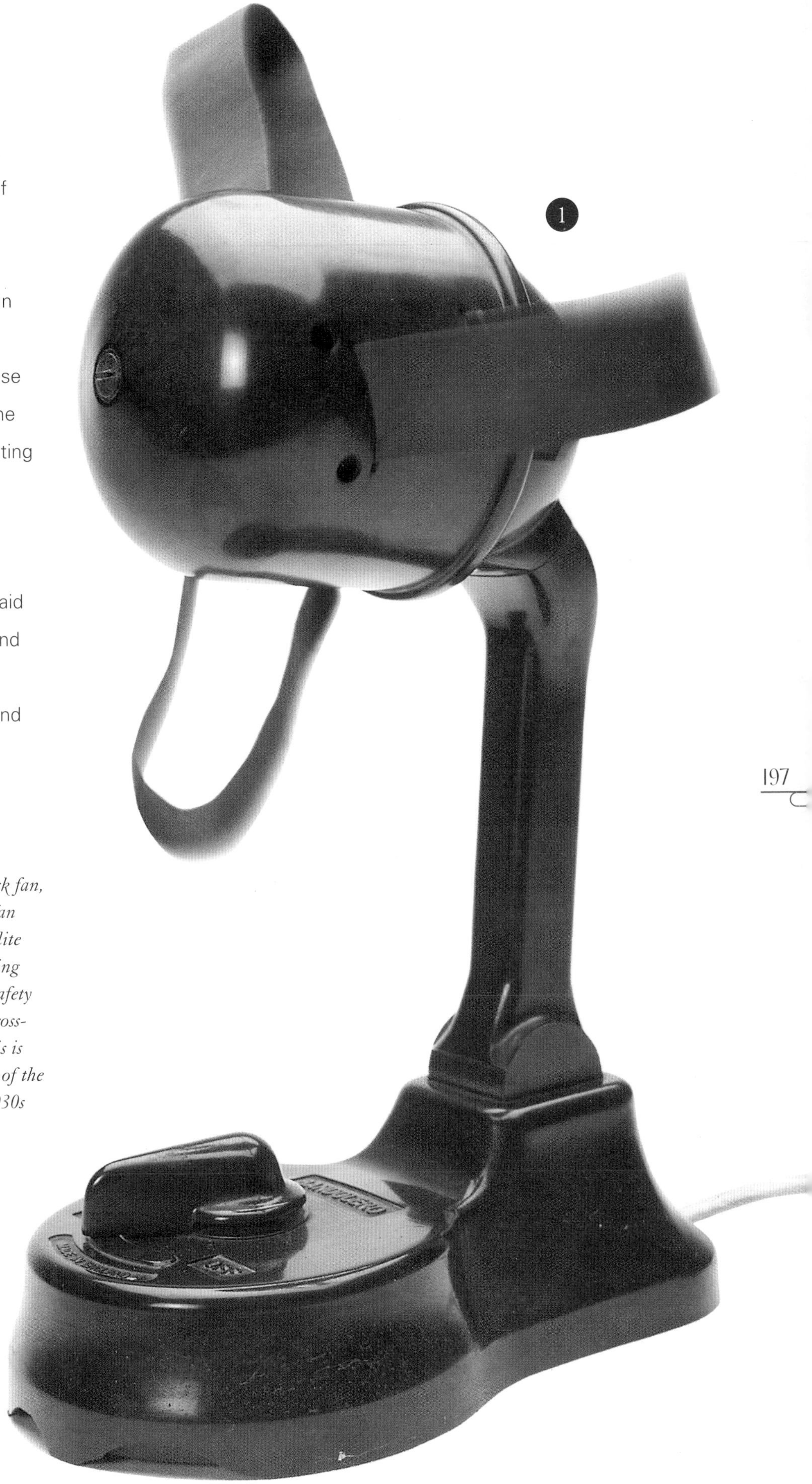

1

1 Bandalero desk fan, by Singer. A fan with an all-Bakelite streamlined housing and replaceable safety blades made of cross-grain ribbon. This is undoubtably one of the finest pieces of 1930s industrial design.

Sunbeam. In 1937, when searching for new products to absorb an overproduction of Bakelite, Philips embarked on the development of a rotary action shaver which was pioneered as the Philishave in 1939.

Plastics were, by their very nature, inherently compatible with the process of streamlining. The flowing lines adapted perfectly to the requirements of plastic-mold design, in which sharp corners and edges were considered structurally weak. In addition, molds with sharp edges generally required expensive hand-finishing. Domed or hemispherical shapes were stronger than flattened ones, since they distributed weight and stress more evenly. A rounded mold also permitted the smooth, even flow of plastic to every corner and surface, and simple tapering lines coupled with an absence of ornamentation made it easy to remove the mold once the object had set. During transport, rounded contours provided protection from breakage and generally enhanced the reflective beauty of glossy plastic. Even as the appeal of streamlining began to fade towards the end of the thirties, the soft, plastic curve persisted in many designs, although with less clearly stated streamlined overtones.

By the mid-forties streamlining had become more restrained. Although immensely popular with the public, the style had attracted a certain amount of criticism for the way in which it hijacked aerodynamic forms and applied them as a purely decorative "sales boosting" style to static consumer goods. The industrial designer Henry Dreyfuss coined the term "cleanlining," which, in his view, better described what designers and manufacturers were attempting to achieve by applying the hallmarks of streamlining to products that "haven't the faintest connection with speed through space."

Cleanlining reflected the increasing vogue for fitness, health, and cleanliness. Domestic items were designed with clean lines and smooth surfaces. Some examples of these new ergonomic forms were Dreyfuss's Hoover vacuum cleaner, Philco's People's Radio Set of 1935–36, the Dairy Maid mixer of 1937, and the 1945 Jumo lamp, one of the most sought-after and collectible streamlined artifacts. Made and patented in France, it combined a molded phenolic shade and base with an articulated chrome and brass arm. Companies were fond of inventing seductive trade names to describe their new products. Titles such as "Aerflow", "Airstream," "Streamform," and "Aero Dynamic" all evocatively conveyed the spirit of the future.

2 Philco People's Set model 444. The export of radios from the US to Britain was hampered by high import duties and other legislation. The streamlined 444 was one of the first to bypass British bureaucracy. The name of the model cleverly exploited the growth of populism in a Depression-hit country.

2
LONG
WAVE
MED
WAVE

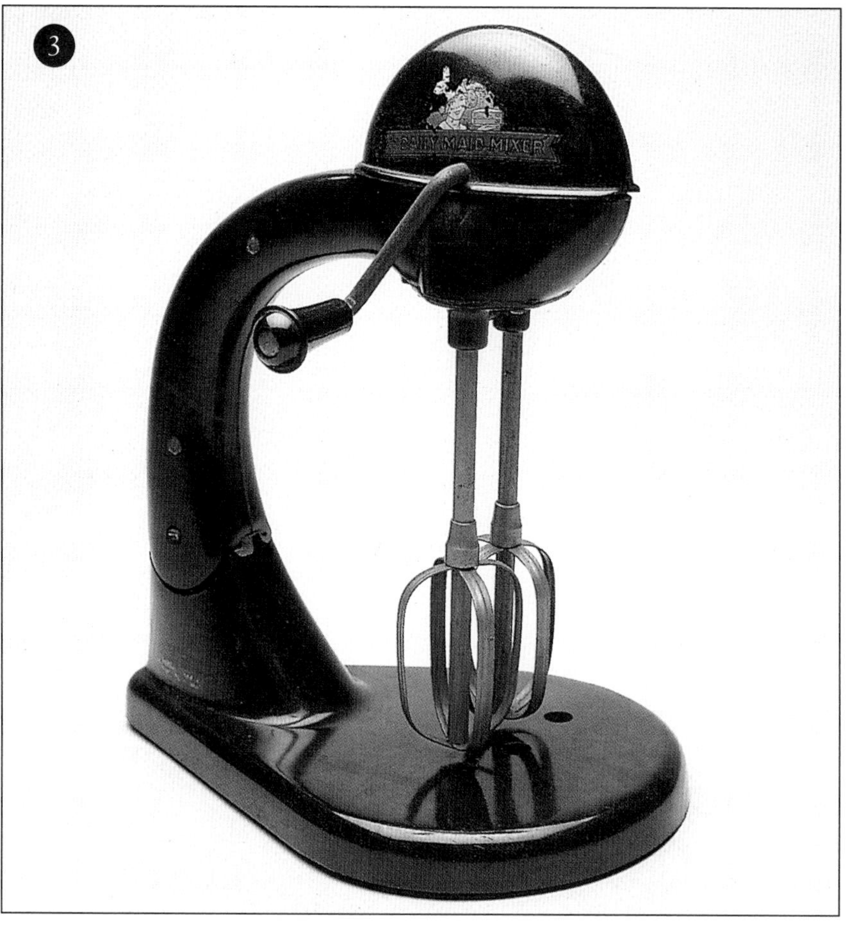

3 *Dairy Maid mixer, by W. A. Deutcher Ltd. An interesting design in which the working mechanisms are hidden within an elegantly functional, easily cleaned body. Bakelite. 1937.*

4 *The Lincoln-Zephyr V-12, advertised in a 1937 issue of Punch, promised the driver "sheer sensuous delight." The teardrop shape arcs nicely over all four wheels.*

The decline of plastics

Following World War II, the enthusiasm which had greeted plastics during the thirties began to wane. Although plastics did comprise a growing percentage of materials used in postwar consumer goods, their reputation as a miracle substance became severely tarnished. After the war, the public wanted "genuine" materials, having grown weary of plastic substitutes, often in poorly conceived applications. To compound matters, war-induced shortages meant that many plastic products were made from poor quality scrap and complaints of "shoddy goods" became commonplace. As the postwar world dawned, the American and European public gradually turned away from Machine Age design back to traditional pseudo-historical styles, which in a time of uncertainty reflected growing nostalgia for a secure past. Although plastics were still widely used, with new varieties being developed and new molding technology continuing to transform the appearance of products, imitation eventually became the order of the day—as it had when the material was first developed at the turn of the century. Traveling full circle, plastic was principally employed for its imitative potential rather than as an expression of technological utopianism.

For Bakelite, the postwar years signaled a retreat from its established position at the forefront of design and technological development. As might be expected, it was gradually superseded in its turn by brighter, stronger, and more flexible materials. By the fifties, the public were demanding brighter acrylics, tougher melamines, and more flexible polythenes. New plastics continued to evolve. The "Britain Can Make It" exhibition and Festival of Britain held in the early fifties demonstrated laminated surfaces made from Warerite and Formica, which were extolled mainly for being easy to clean. The vision of the early plastics pioneers had been disappointingly condensed into what the American cultural historian Jeffrey L. Meikle called "damp-cloth utopianism."

After the war, a stigma had become attached to Bakelite which it never quite succeeded in shaking off. The dull, "somber" colors, the queer smell and the lingering overtones of utility were distinctly at odds with the bright, clean, brave new world of the fifties and sixties. No longer in demand for consumer goods, Bakelite returned mercurial career ending as it had begun, with the distributor cap and rotor blade.

It was in the thirties that Bakelite had truly come of age as a material with an appreciable identity for the consumer. During this exciting period, designers and manufacturers used Bakelite to extend the limits of creative freedom and explore new possibilities. Despite its subsequent fall from grace, the manufacturing frenzy of the thirties has left a huge legacy of extraordinary objects for collectors to seek out and cherish. Perhaps, in retrospect, "a thousand uses" could be regarded as something of an understatement!

Collecting

Collecting radios

Bakelite moldings that have been formed by heat-and-pressure are rigid, brittle, heavy, fairly thick, and have a hard feel, are always opaque and could only be made in dull colors: mostly brown or black, less often in dark reds and greens. They can be plain or mottled to simulate mahogany or walnut. These colors are not just on the surface like paint, so look inside to check that the color goes all the way through. Occasionally, ordinary brown Bakelite was used, then sprayed over with brighter colors, but not all such painted sets are genuine: painting sometimes indicates that recent repairs have been concealed.

Catalin-type cabinets which are made by pouring resin mixtures into molds have a softer, more flexible feel about them and are more easily cracked, worn, and scratched than hard Bakelite ones. They are also more translucent and can be in bright, jewel-like hues which may change color with prolonged exposure to ultraviolet light and will distort if subjected to heat and sunlight. Blues turn to dark greens with age and white goes yellow but this can be corrected by an expert. Often, tops have burn marks caused by the hot valves inside which cannot be removed.

The Catalin-type cabinets are perhaps more easily confused with modern plastics by the novice but when you have become familiar with them, you will find them unmistakable and will be able to spot fakes.

Check that knobs, plastic and chromium decoration pieces, dials, and glasses are original, as these are being reproduced, although you may find them more acceptable than non-matching ones from other sets.

In judging a prospective purchase, try to inspect the inside too for repair patches and signs of corrosion due to dampness. And use a trained nose as well as your expert eye to check for signs of overheating that could mean an expensive electrical overhaul. Examine the cloth that covers the loudspeaker aperture: if it doesn't look in the same condition as the rest of the set, it may be a replacement. This may be acceptable if a good match to an original one.

Since Bakelite radios are now becoming expensive, you would be advised to insure your collection and protect it with some security measures. Some Art Deco radios cost several thousand dollars apiece. At a London auction not long ago, a rare Round Ekco in imitation green marble—which puzzled some experts—fetched almost $26,500, which compares with about $665 for an identical plain brown one. Such freak results rarely set precedents; if another appears, it is likely to fetch a great deal less,

particularly since such events spark off a spate of reproductions making potential buyers wary.

But what is a radio worth? That, as any dealer will tell you, is simply a matter of how much collectors are willing to pay. Prices are mostly established at auctions and by dealers who are able to charge "what the market will bear." There is an approximate standard price for many radios which is based on "good condition" but "mint" examples may fetch a third more and "poor" but still original and complete ones only half that, while cracked, broken, or incomplete ones may be unsalable except to pirate for spare parts. Changing fashions and fads also cause price fluctuations among fickle collectors who like to change their love-objects often, so today's bargain can easily become tomorrow's worst buy.

You should have your collection properly valued for insurance purposes. If you are a good customer, your radio dealer may help you with this—but you should not necessarily expect an expert to give you the benefit of his knowledge free of charge. Auctioneers will give free valuations of items you may intend to put up for auction but these may not match store prices or "insurance value" which takes into account the price of a rapid replacement. Don't underinsure, but there is no point in overinsuring either, since you will only be paid the "current market value" at the time of replacement.

It is a good idea to put "invisible ink" security markings on things to help identify them if stolen and to photograph them, writing details on the back of the prints to build up a pocket album of your collection.

Ekco Model AC85, by E. K. Cole Ltd. Known affectionately as the "Dougal Set," this radio, the precursor to the Wells-Coates Ekco, seems rather clumsy and old-fashioned. It was made in Bakelite in 1934.

Don't plug it in

After you have made your purchase—what next? Do you immediately plug the radio into an outlet and wait for it to blow a fuse, or possibly burst into flames if you have not checked the voltage is the same as your supply? The answer is "No." If you are not technically minded, do not fiddle with it or you could get a dangerous shock, or indeed blow it up. Get an expert to check it first. If the set works, you should still treat it with care: do not let young children near it and do not operate it in damp places like kitchens and bathrooms because it is highly unlikely to conform to today's safety standards.

There are other questions you should ask yourself. Is the radio a battery set? Are you still able to obtain batteries? What voltage does it require? Does it work on AC or DC? What does "60 cycles" mean? Does it require an aerial? Should it be earthed? If you do not know the answers, take advice from a reliable source rather than take risks.

Wherever you find your radios, it is important to bear in mind that many countries now have tough safety laws concerning electrical items which forbid the sale and use of equipment that does not comply with modern safety standards. It is unlikely that any vintage radios—except battery-operated ones—will comply with such regulations, so responsible professionals who trade in them are likely to take the necessary precautions. They may render the radio inoperable by removing the electric cord or other components; or they may adapt the set to make it safe to use; or may simply snip off the plug and sell it as "antique apparatus for display and research only" (the latter strategy may not protect them from the law).

Will your radio work?

When you buy a vintage Bakelite radio, you should remember that broadcasting has changed very much since it was designed. Old radios will usually only tune-in programs broadcast on the original AM (Amplitude Modulation) system on long, medium, and short wavebands which are often shown on the dial of the set. These receivers will not tune-in stations broadcasting on the FM (Frequency Modulation) system introduced in recent times—which you will not find marked on the dials of early receivers. Sometimes, particular stations may at present be broadcasting on the old AM systems as well as FM and in this case you may be lucky enough to be able to get your favorite program but if not, you will have to put up with whatever is available. It is not feasible to convert such sets to FM but you might be able to get a separate converter. Alternatively, you could feed the set with music to match its age from a hidden cassette-recorder with the help of an electronic engineer: the trick with this is to tell your friends you have bought an old radio that still gets old sounds and to astonish them with a demonstration.

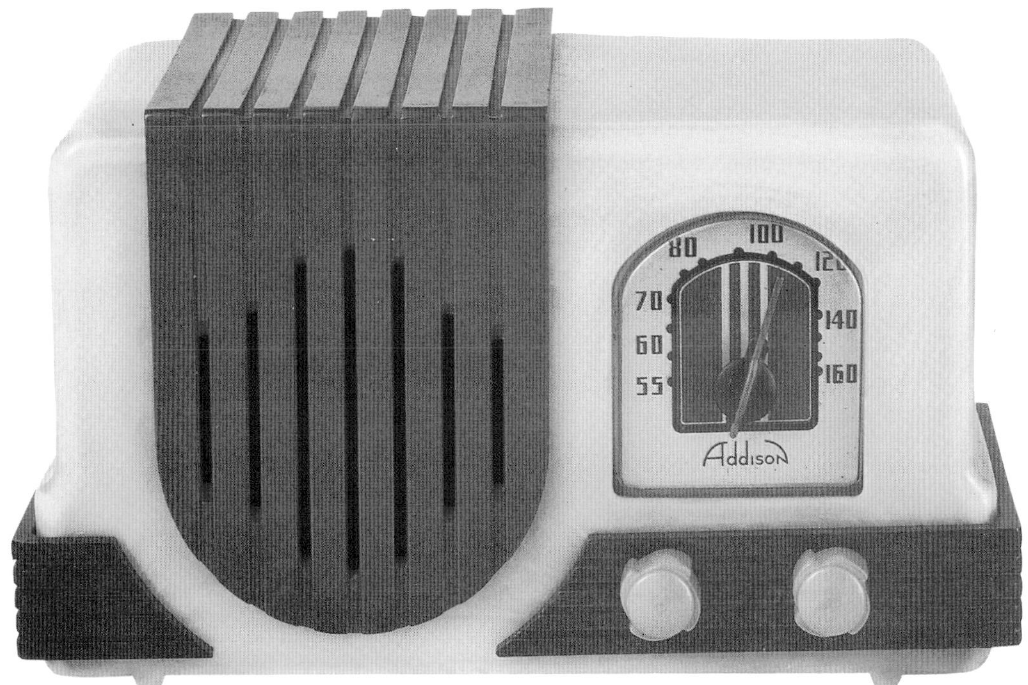

With its wonderful cascading waterfall grille, the Canadian Addison of 1940 came in a large variety of solid and marbleized color combinations. Made in either Catalin or Plaskon, this gorgeous red-and-yellow Catalin example is one of the most sought color combinations.

Collecting jewelry

The first step in collecting Bakelite jewelry is to find a dealer who: has a large inventory of at least 100 pieces of Bakelite (if they have other plastics also, this is an extra feather in their cap); has a fair knowledge of the different plastics; and will take the time and trouble to help you in your quest for knowledge.

Spend some time with this person. Have them show you how to get the phenol smell by rubbing the piece hard and fast as though you wanted to raise a blister. When your thumb becomes very hot, smell it quickly—the odor will dissipate in about two seconds.

When you have accomplished this, the next move is to buy a group of several bangles or other pieces. Explain to the dealer you want to do some experimenting at home. Vary your selection according to the types of plastic: some Bakelite, celluloid, and acrylics (Lucite), and spend as little as you can. Label the bracelets or pins as to their composition so that you will be able to decipher which is which at a later time.

When you get your purchases home you can set up your area for experimenting. If space is tight, go to a hardware store or lumber yard and purchase a sheet of plywood about 2 feet x 2 feet, or 2 feet x 4 feet, to provide you with a mobile work area. Next you will want a couple of small boxes in which to store the bracelets and the following tools: a toothbrush (very stiff); pliers (flat jaw, not serrated or tongs); a small sharp knife; a hacksaw blade (fine-toothed); and assorted grit sandpaper (200, 400, 600).

You can add to your tools as you go along, but these will do for now. You may also want to set up your work space near the hot-water faucet or a stove to boil water.

Take your Bakelite piece and run it under your hottest faucet water, for about 30 seconds, and smell quickly. This should release the phenol smell. If not, dip your piece into boiling water and smell it again. If the piece is really Bakelite or another phenolic, you will get an odor.

The next step is to take the pieces that you have labeled celluloid and acrylic and dip these. At extremely hot temperatures you may pick up a slightly camphor smell from the celluloid, and a smell somewhat similar to automobile oil from the acrylic. If the water is not very hot, you will not register any odor. Once you get this phenol odor you will never forget it.

Once the items have cooled, you may want to try the thumb-rubbing test on each piece. This should be done after the articles have been in hot water, so that you can melt all the layers of wax and polish off each piece before testing. Once stripped of its polish and wax coatings, Bakelite has an abrasive feel. Your thumb will heat up rather quickly with Bakelite, and other plastics will feel more slippery to the touch. Again, you will also smell the phenolic-resin odor from Bakelite, whereas you will never attain a smell from cooled thermoplastics.

Take the different pieces, and drop them together into a container of hot water for about three to five minutes. Being careful not to scald yourself, retrieve them with pliers or tongs, and as soon as they are cool enough to handle but still hot, try to bend, twist, and knead them. Thermoplastics will become pliable and thermoset phenolics will remain rigid.

Stack of clear and opaque polka-dotted bangles.

Another experiment is to hold a Bakelite piece lightly between your thumb and forefinger and gently tap it, if possible, with another piece of Bakelite. The resulting sound is similar to the tapping of two pieces of bamboo; a dull, hollow, thud. When the same thing is done with other plastics, you get more of a higher-pitched, clacking sound. This method will come in handy when you are more experienced. When you have a bangle that you know is Bakelite but the sound is not quite there, you may find, on closer inspection, that the bangle has a crack or has been repaired. Cast bangles seem to have a tempered-like quality, and when cracked or repaired never regain that bamboo sound. Remember this, as it will save you spending money on pieces that you may discover later have been damaged or repaired.

Finally, ask yourself, "Is it old or newly made?" There is a particular reason for the careful wording of this question. It could have

Various clear colored bangles.

been, "Is it old or new Bakelite?" This is similar to asking, "Is it old or new amber?"

Amber, in order to evolve into its present form, has let nature take the sap from a tree and compress and petrify it for thousands of years, or more. How do you classify anything that old as new? Granted, cuttings and sweepings from the work area are ground up and sold as reprocessed amber, but it is still amber.

Bakelite is similar. All the Bakelite jewelry that you see today is old Bakelite. It was cast from the mid-twenties up until the early forties when the formula was sold to Union Carbide. The Marblette company produced until the early fifties. There isn't any company producing cast-phenolic jewelry today, because of the cost. They would first

The activity of collecting plastics has changed greatly over the last twenty years. In the past stallholders and antique dealers were only too eager to dispense with "virtually unsalable" plastic artifacts. Such attitudes were responsible for the casual destruction of large quantities of Bakelite objects on the grounds that they were commonplace and therefore essentially worthless. Paradoxically, as a result of this blinkered thinking, Bakelite became increasingly rare and ultimately began to assume some kind of value—although it was not until fairly recently that pieces began to appear in auction rooms. Today, the importance of vintage plastics is widely acknowledged, and such artifacts have become collectible in their own right.

have to acquire the resins. The extreme heat-and-pressure process used to cast the phenolics is too costly. The machines, jigs, and vacuum systems (the fine dust produced in carving has to be collected so that it is not ingested) used to carve the pieces, as well as the tumblers to polish them, have mostly gone to the boneyard.

In recent years there has been an increasing proliferation of reproduction Bakelite objects, which inevitably presents a problem for the serious collector. Furthermore, unlike silver or porcelain, Bakelite has no characteristic maker's mark to act as a guide and thus even experts can experience difficulties with identification. In general, Bakelite is recognizable by its weight (heavier than modern plastics and celluloids); color (limited range of dark colors); patina; and feel. Familiarity and experience are the best tools, so you should take every opportunity to examine, study and handle Bakelite objects. Bakelite is a very tactile material and can manifest itself in a wide range of surfaces. You can also confirm identification by what is known as the "hot pin" test. If a heated pin does not penetrate the surface of an object (do this in well-ventilated surroundings) then it is genuine phenolic. There is also the characteristic odor of carbolic soap—heated or wet, Bakelite smells of carbolic soap, which contains phenol-carbolic acid. Obviously the hot pin test has certain practical drawbacks, in that it is usually only possible to carry it out after you have purchased an object. Not surprisingly, attempts to explain the purpose of such a procedure to a seller may meet with some opposition, but if it is possible to test prior to purchase, always do so on the underside of an object, as a precaution against any unnecessary damage.

You would be unlikely to find a business manager today who would recommend that his company retool and incur the kind of expense it would take to indulge a whim that is restricted to the antiques and collectibles field.

The long and the short of it is that the bulk of what is called "new Bakelite" is in fact another polymer. The difference can be detected in many ways. The presence of the color white is an immediate indicator. There is no longer a white-colored Bakelite.

If you take a Bakelite mah-jong cube (generally a light yellow to mustard color) and cut it slightly with your hacksaw blade, you will find a brilliant, white stripe where you did your cutting.

Put the mah-jong piece on a sun-exposed windowsill for a month or two, and see if the altered area doesn't change, so that you barely notice where the cut was. If you take a piece of Bakelite jewelry, and find an inconspicuous area to sand with your 200 grit paper you will be amazed. You will find that mustard will turn to white. Some of the weird, dark green colors will lighten to a rich cobalt. Some of the lighter oranges will shine a pastel pink. Dark greens turn a light jade color and a light greenish orange reveals a light blue. These are colors that some of the most adamant collectors have yet to behold. If you finish the sanded area with 600 grit paper and leave it on your windowsill, in thirty days you will be hard pressed to figure out where you sanded.

Bangles and napkin rings demonstrate

this color change process. If you look inside then outside, you will find the inner areas much lighter than the exposed outer ones. The same is true with the fronts and backs of other pieces.

Over time you will find quite a few examples of items newly manufactured from old pieces of Bakelite. There are people who comb the old findings warehouses throughout the country, in search of old Bakelite parts. These are generally found at flea markets, dangling on modern chains. Some buttons are made into earrings. There are all kinds of pieces that are utilized and sold as finished products. The best way to tell these is to look at the findings or fastenings used. Most of these pieces have findings (purchased at the local craft shop) hot-glued or superglued onto an old piece of Bakelite. Neither of these adhesives existed at the time when the Bakelite was produced. What you want to see, if you are looking for original construction, is a pin-back that is two separate components, set into holes drilled into the plastic. Another construction to look for is two tabs on the back of the pin-back, pressed into holes that were drilled at back angles and pressed back into the angle of the holes. A third is a bar pin that has rivets or screws fastening the pin to the body.

Giveaways for necklaces are the chains. Most neckware used the celluloid chains of the twenties and thirties, with some American and many German designers utilizing solid brass chains. Some French designers used chromium-plated brass and copper for chains as well as accent parts. If the chains do not fall into one of these categories, you should take a much closer look. You will also see jewelry that was made from gaming pieces—for example, mah-jong and domino bracelets, with pins and earrings that match.

This is an example of fruity earrings at their lurid best. Made of bright red and green cast phenolic, 1940s.

Care and maintenance

Bakelite is generally easy to care for, but can, over time, be susceptible to bleaching by strong sunlight, which breaks down the surface sheen, to give an overall matt appearance. Evidence of bleaching is also manifested by a contrasting intensity of color on inner and outer surfaces. When this condition has occurred, it is difficult to rectify. Once the surface loses its initial layer of polish, the phenolic material develops a seemingly unquenchable thirst for polishes, oils, and lacquers which require to be assiduously applied. You can apply a cellulose coating to restore the surface sheen, but this is generally inadvisable since the cellulose layer is very superficial. When arranging pieces on display, therefore, avoid placing them in direct sunlight. For general-purpose cleaning of objects, certain brands of metal polish may be used. The plastics historian Sylvia Katz recommends Mister Sheen and Johnson's Wax Sparkle.

Painted Bakelite presents further problems. The presence of paint leads to the suspicion that an indifferent specimen has been "made over" in order to boost its price. Underneath the paint is an unknown quantity which may or may not justify the outlay. It is worth bearing in mind that layers of paint on phenolic tables and radio cabinets may sometimes conceal deep scratches. Any attempt to remove the paint, which can become defiantly embedded in the scratches, is likely to damage the original glossy surface beneath.

This plaque by Clang Ltd bears a message from Edward VIII announcing his abdication.

Price is also an important consideration. Sometimes it may be necessary to pay a higher than usual price to secure a perfect specimen. Usually this is not a source of regret to bona fide collectors. There is also the question of rarity value. If an object appears to be particularly unusual, then it may be worth accepting it in less than perfect condition. Minor cracks, chips, or blemishes can sometimes be repaired or disguised, but some collectors prefer to leave well alone, taking the view that the odd scratch is a manifestation of the object's past life and such minor flaws merely serve to enhance its character.

Discovered among a selection of irons in an auction, the function of the Roll-a-Ray by the Sutton Corporation remains a mystery! The streamlined body holds a light bulb and is propelled along on rubber wheels, ultimately designed to massage your back. Made from phenolic and rubber in the late 1930s.

Radios

If you need to repair or restore your radio, take care or you may ruin it. Museums aim to conserve and preserve rather than to restore or repair objects. They are concerned with keeping things in safe conditions and adopt the policy. "Do nothing that cannot be reversed," so if it is decided to deal with cabinet damage for instance, removable wax rather than anything permanent would be used. Any changes made are recorded on a label for future historians. Your maxim should be "If in doubt—leave it alone." If you decide to do repairs and restoration, take some safety precautions before starting work. Wear protective clothing and use a mask and goggles if using harmful solvents, abrasives, and electric tools.

If the radio is undamaged and works, it may simply need a gentle cleaning and for this you can use a mild detergent solution followed by a good wax polish—but do not get water inside it and make sure it is unplugged before starting work. If you need to remove the works, remove screws carefully and make a note of where everything goes for reassembly.

On display, some cabinets seem to attract dust, so using an antistatic polish may help to keep it clean. Brownish-yellow discoloration often results from a sticky deposit of tars from tobacco smoke which can be removed with detergent; but if you are a smoker, you may have already considered giving it up to finance your new collecting habit.

Its offset pointer, large flat expanse of Catalin, and unusual color make this Sentinel of 1939 stand out. This model is both rare and desirable, especially intact as it has a very great tendency to crack.

A set which is badly soiled may require the use of special abrasive polishes but in this case begin with the most gentle kind because shiny surfaces are often a very thin skin which if broken may expose a rough core that can never be polished. Paint spots can be removed with a plastic scraper or diluted chemical stripper which should be first tested for corrosiveness on an unseen area. Cracks can be filled with colored wax of the sort used by furniture restorers and broken-off pieces can be secured with an epoxy resin glue. If you possess the sort of skills which car repairers have, you will be able to fill in missing areas with material used in their trade—but you will need to dye it to match first. Experts use cold-casting resins, some of which can be bought ready-made, to mold missing parts like knobs, dial surrounds, and decorative appliqué. Different techniques are needed according to the type of cabinet material. The most difficult to repair are the Catalin types which are translucent, so almost any repair will show.

The acquisition, study, restoration, care, and usage of Bakelite radios are very important matters, whatever the purpose of the collector: whether a hobbyist, homemaker, aesthete, technician, designer, historian, or museum curator. But further studies which consider the objects in their social, psychological, and domestic contexts will greatly enrich the enjoyment and importance of the collection of any radiophile.

Jewelry

Whenever you find a piece for your collection, give it a hot soapy bath. Clean all the road dirt and layers of whatever off with an old toothbrush, then give the piece a nice towel-drying. Now apply a healthy amount of polish and scrub away.

Simi-Chrome seems to be most commonly used but Top Bright will do just as well. Both come from Germany and smell, feel, and work the same. If you go to an auto-body supplier, you may be able to pick up a gallon of rubbing or polishing compound for the same price as a small tube of the others. Using a toothbrush and the mixture of your choice, work rigorously into all the nooks and crannies. Remove all excess polish by scrubbing well under very cold water. The last step; using an old towel, buff out your piece until you achieve a uniform rich luster.

Your pieces should be stored away from direct sunlight and, when transported, should be wrapped up in soft paper, or cloth, and not allowed to rub or bang against each other; the result could be dull abrasion marks, or even chips.

These beautifully colored large dice must be purely decorative, as it is hard to imagine someone actually rolling these whoppers! Made from cast-phenolic resin, probably in the 1940s.

Bibliography

Aitken, Professor Hugh. *Syntony and Spark.* USA: 1977.

Arts Council. *The Thirties—British Art and Design before the War*. London: 1979.

Baker, W. J. *A History of the Marconi Company*. London: Methuen, 1970.

Banham, Reyner. *Theory and Design in the First Machine Age.*

Barthes, R. *Mythologies.* Vintage, 1993.

BBC Handbooks and Yearbooks. London: 1928 onward.

Bergonzi, B. *Old Gramophones.* Shire, 1991.

Biraud, Guy. *Les Radio Philips de Collection.*

Biraud, Guy. *Guide du Collectionneur* and *La Restauration et la Conservation.* France: 1987.

Boselli, Primo. *Il Museo Della Radio.* Florence: Edizioni Medicea, 1989.

Briggs, Asa. *The History of Broadcasting in the UK.* Oxford: Oxford University Press, 1961–79.

Briggs, Susan. *Those Radio Times.* London: Weidenfield and Nicholson, 1981.

Britt, David (Ed.). *Modern Art Impressionism to Post-Modernism.* London: Thames and Hudson, 1989.

Bunis, Marty and Sue. *Collector's Guide to Antique Radios.* USA: Collector Books (Schroeder), 1991.

Burrows, Arthur. *The Story of Broadcasting.* 3 vols, London: Cassell PLC, Publishing, 1924.

Cabinet Maker, The. London: 1930–3.

Carrington, Noel. *British Achievement in Design.* London: 1946.

Chew, V. K. *Talking Machines.* London: Science Museum, 1967.

Claricoats, John. *The World At Their Fingertips.* London: RSGB, 1967.

Collins, Michael. *Towards Post-Modernism.* London: British Museum, 1987.

Constable, Anthony. *Early Wireless.* London: Midas, 1980.

Cook, Patrick and **Slessor**, Catherine. *Bakelite, An Illustrated Guide to Collectible Bakelite Objects.* London: The Apple Press, 1992.

Dalton, W. M. *The Story of Radio.* 2 vols, Inst. of Physics, 1975.

De Vries, Leonard. *Victorian Inventions.* London: John Murray, 1971.

DiNoto, Andrea. *Art Plastic, Design for Living.* Abbeyville, 1984.

Douglas, Alan. *Radio Manufacturers.* Several volumes, New York: 1988 onwards.

Eckersley, Peter. *The Power Behind the Microphone.* London: Jonathan Cape, 1941.

Eisler, Paul. *My Life with the Printed Circuit.* AUP, 1989.

Ernst Erb. *Radio von Gestern.* Switzerland: M+K Computer Verlag AG.

Forester, Tom (Ed.). *Microelectronics Revolution.* Oxford: Blackwell, 1980.

Forty, Adrian. *Objects of Desire.* London: Thames and Hudson, 1986.

Forty, Adrian. "Wireless Style", *Architectural Association Quarterly*, vol. 4. 1972.

Freud, Sigmund. *The Interpretation of Dreams.* Standard Edition, London: Pelican, 1976.

Freud, Sigmund. *The Psychopathology of Everyday Life.* London: Pelican, 1976.

Grinder, Robert and **Fathauer**, George. *Radio Directory.* USA: 1986.

Ham, Ron and **Rudram**, David. *History of Communications.* Amberley Industrial History Museum.

Hawes, Robert (Ed.). *Bulletin of the British Vintage Wireless Society.* London: 1982–1994.

Hawes, Robert. *Radio Art.* London: Greenwood, 1991.

Harmsworth Wireless Encyclopedia, c1923.

Heskett, John. *Industrial Design.* London: Thames and Hudson, 1980.

Humphries, Lund. *Eye for Industry.* London: Royal Society for Arts, 1986.

International Design Yearbooks. London: Thames and Hudson.

Jenson, Peter R. *In Marconi's Footsteps—Early Radio.* Australia: Kangaroo Press, 1994.

Jessop, George. *The Bright Sparks of Radio.* London: RSGB, 1990.

Johnson, David and Betty. *Antique Radios and Guide to Old Radios.* USA: Wallace-Homestead, 1982 and 1989.

Jung, Carl. *Man and his Symbols.* London: Aldus/Jupiter, 1964/74.

Katz, Sylvia. *Classic Plastics.* London: Thames and Hudson, 1984.

Katz, Sylvia (Ed.) *The Plastics Age.* London: Victoria and Albert Museum, 1990.

Katz, Sylvia. *Early Plastics.* London: Octopus, 1974.

Klein, Dan. *Art Deco.* London: Octopus, 1974.

L'e Turner, Gerard. *19th Century Scientific Instruments.* London: Sothebys/Philip Wilson, 1983.

Lethaby, W. *Form in Civilisation.* London: 1922.

Littmann, Frederic. "The evolution of the wireless receiver," *Design for Today* magazine. March 1936.

Lodge, Sir Oliver. *Talks about Wireless.* London: Cassell, 1925.

Long, Joan. *A First Class Job.* Murphy, 1985.

MacKenzie, Donald and **Wajcman**, Judy. *The Industrial Revolution in the Home.* Oxford: Oxford University Press, 1985.

Miller, Charles. *Practical handbook of valve radio repair.* London: Newnes, 1982.

O'Dea, *Handbook: Radio Communications Collections.* London: Science Museum, 1934.

O'Neill, Amanda (Ed.). *Introduction to the Decorative Arts.* London: Tiger, 1990.

Packard, Vance. *The Hidden Persuaders.* London: Longmans, 1957.

Paul, Floyd. *Radio horn speaker encyclopedia.* USA: 1987.

Pevsner, Nikolaus. *Enquiry into the state of Industrial Art in England.* Cambridge: Cambridge University Press, 1937.

Pevsner, Nikolaus. *Pioneers of Modern Design.* New York Museum of Modern Art, 1949.

Pevsner, Nikolaus. "The Radio Cabinet," *Architectural Review.* London: May 1940.

Povey, P. J. and **Earl**, R. A. J. *Vintage Telephones.* London: Peregrinus/London Science Museum, IEE, 1988.

Proudfoot, Christopher. *Collecting Phonographs and Gramophones.* London: Christies/Vista, 1980.

Rowlands, Dr Peter and **Wilson**, Dr Patrick. *Oliver Lodge and the Invention of Radio.* Liverpool: P. D. Publications, 1994.

Royal Academy. *50 Years of the Bauhaus.* London: 1968.

Russell, Gordon. *The Designer's Trade.* London: 1968. Also articles in *Design for Today* magazine, 1933.

Sideli, John. *Classic Plastic Radios.* New York: Dutton, 1990.

Soresini, Franco. *La Radio.* Milan: BE-MA Editrice, 1988.

Sparke, Penny. *An Introduction to Design and Culture in the Twentieth Century.* London: Allen and Unwin, 1986.

Sparke, Penny. *The Plastics Age, From Modernity to Post-Modernity.* London: Victoria and Albert Museum, 1990.

Stokes, John. *The Golden Age of Radio in the Home.* New Zealand: 1986, and further volume.

Stokes, John. *70 Years of Radio Tubes.*

Sturmey, S. G. *The Economic Development of Radio.* London: Duckworth, 1958.

Tyne, Gerald. *Saga of the Vacuum Tube.* USA.

Van de Lemme, Arie. *A Guide to Art Deco Style.* Magna Books: 1992.

Wander, Tim. *2MT Writtle: The Birth of British Broadcasting.* Chelmsford: Capella, 1988.

Ward, Peter. *Kitsch in Sync—A Consumer's Guide to Bad Taste.* London: Plexus, 1991.

Whiteley, Nigel. "Toward a Throwaway Culture," *Oxford Art Journal*, vol. 10. 1987.

Wyborn, E. J. and **Landauer**, W. *Plastics and Trend.* London: Summer 1936.

Index

Picture Credits: t=top b=bottom l=left r = right c=center

Christie's: pp64, 70, 86bl; Alastair Duncan/collection Mitchell Wolfson Jnr, Miami Dade Community College: p39b; Macdonald/Aldus Archive: pp5, 39t; James Meehan: pp87b, 93t; Robert Opie: p199; Plastics Historical Society: pp34t, 34r; Quarto Publishing plc: p171; Gad Sassower: pp5cl, 16, 18bl, 18br, 19, 21b, 38, 40, 42b, 46br, 50, 51, 52t, 53t, 54, 55r, 57, 58br, 61tr, 61b, 71, 80, 111, 118r, 126, 127, 195tl, 213, 217; Rudiger Walz: p123.